Heroes & VILLAINS
of
NOTTINGHAM

ADAM NIGHTINGALE

Heroes & VILLAINS
of
NOTTINGHAM

ADAM NIGHTINGALE

To June Hammond

First published 2009

The History Press
The Mill, Brimscombe Port
Stroud, Gloucestershire, GL5 2QG
www.thehistorypress.co.uk

© Adam Nightingale, 2009

The right of Adam Nightingale to be identified as the Author
of this work has been asserted in accordance with the
Copyrights, Designs and Patents Act 1988.

British Library Cataloguing in Publication Data.
A catalogue record for this book is available from the British Library.

ISBN 978 0 7524 4924 1

Typesetting and origination by The History Press
Printed in Great Britain

Contents

Acknowledgements & Credits

Thanks to Susannah Nightingale, Laura Dean, Steve and Rachel Roberts, Bev Baker, Laura Butler, the Galleries of Justice, and Nick Tomlinson of Picture the Past. Thanks also to Cate Ludlow, Matilda Richards and Alexander Bud at The History Press.

Action illustrations by Stephen Dennis. Portraits by Jean Nightingale. Pictures of the Luddite, the razor, and the pistol by Peter Nightingale. Photographs by Mark Nightingale (with additional images taken by the author). Archive photographs courtesy of Nottingham County Council, G.H.F. Atkins, the Thoroton Society of Nottinghamshire, and www.picturethepast.org.uk.

Introduction

Why No Robin Hood?

A year and a half before the publication of this book I wrote an overview of Nottingham's criminal history called *Murder & Crime: Nottingham*. In that book I assiduously avoided the temptation to do a chapter on Robin Hood. I went even further and made certain that there was no mention of Robin Hood, even in passing, in the pages of the book. *Heroes & Villains of Nottingham* similarly refuses to profile or namecheck the outlaw. Even in the chapter exploring the feud between King Richard and his brother John, the respective benefactor and nemesis of Robin Hood, the man in green's name isn't mentioned once. So why do it? If Nottingham is known internationally for anything, surely it's Robin Hood? That's partly the point for his exclusion. It shouldn't be this way, but Robin Hood's ubiquity seems always to be at the expense of a local history that is as rich and colourful, sinister and dramatic as any other city in the country. There should be room for both, but that doesn't seem to be the case. Generally speaking, Nottingham is defined by the outlaw to the exclusion of most other historical considerations. So, Robin Hood's omission is a way of redressing the balance and drawing attention to a local history that, rather than being parochial, was disproportionately pivotal in shaping England.

The other, slightly more obvious reason for Robin Hood's exclusion is the fact that all the figures in this book actually existed. None of them are composites of four or five sketchy historical characters. None of them are mythological figures, and most of them are largely forgotten. How did I choose them? I am indebted to R. Mellors' *Men of Nottingham and Nottinghamshire*, an out of print who's who of local heroes bought from the indispensable Oxfam bookshop in West Bridgeford. It's a wildly inaccurate book that gratuitously claims at least one other Yorkshireman who doesn't belong to Nottingham. However, it made me aware of Edward Fenton, the Elizabethan Privateer who was a supporting player in two of the era's great maritime adventures and the Puritan soldier Captain John Hutchinson, who tore down Nottingham Castle in the aftermath of the English Civil War. These were the first two chapters I wrote and the spur to hunt down or flesh out all the rest of the soldiers, killers, activists and aristocrats who appear in the book, everyone of them compelling enough to share that plinth greedily occupied by a man in green reluctant to divide his glory with many deserving heroes and villains.

There is no doubt that all the characters included in these pages deserve their place here, however, should they be classed as heroes or villains? That is for you to decide.

ONE

A Child with Bad Companions

King John and Nottingham Castle

In 1194 the full weight of the medieval war machine descended on Nottingham. The great warrior, King Richard I, had returned to England. He had come in person to the small Midlands town to suppress a rebellion orchestrated by his younger brother, John. He had stopped briefly at Canterbury, spent a night in London attending a religious service at St Paul's Cathedral, and then headed north. John was in France, but his supporters were in possession of two impressive castles that were difficult to storm: Tickhill and Nottingham. Tickhill surrendered without a fight. As Richard marched across England, most of John's supporters faded into the background. Only the rebels at Nottingham had the courage to continue to openly defy their lawful King.

In late March Richard entered Nottingham at the head of a large and heavily armed body of men. The castle defenders were unnerved by the sound of war trumpets and the number of soldiers that had come against them. In spite of the terrible misgivings that they must have felt they held their resolve and prepared for the initial assault.

Richard was believed to have led the first attack himself. As dusk fell the King was said to have personally killed a defender, shooting him dead with an arrow. Within a few hours Richard's forces had taken the castle's wooden outer defences and burned them, but had failed to breach the stone fortifications. Richard's forces had also taken prisoners. That night the defenders retaliated by starting fires of their own among Richard's defensive works.

The following day Richard's response was twofold. He hanged prisoners in full view of the rebels and threatened the castle with his war machinery. Richard had at his disposal powerful and exotic siege weapons.

King John.

During the siege of Nottingham Castle Richard I shot a defender dead with an arrow.

He ordered two of his catapults to be brought into Nottingham. The King was also in possession of Greek fire, the agonisingly painful liquid flame weapon used by the Saracen armies he had fought against in the Holy Land. Richard's actions that morning were a deliberate flexing of muscle designed to undermine the resolve of the rebels and avoid a protracted and needlessly bloody siege. It seemed to work. A small delegation of rebel knights requested permission to speak with the King. Richard granted their request. He encouraged the knights to return to the castle and persuade their brothers-in-arms to surrender. There must have been a promise of clemency from the King as he talked with his rebellious subjects because, the following day, the defenders laid down their weapons and the siege, which had only lasted a few days, was over. Richard permitted all the knights who had surrendered to go free on condition that they paid ransoms. Their subordinates were not so fortunate. Richard hanged the rebel sergeants. He also made brutal examples of two local and influential civilians who had openly supported the rebellion, starving one of them to death and flaying the other alive.

On 29 March, the day after the siege had concluded, Richard went hunting in Sherwood Forest. On 30 March he applied himself to the less exhilarating business of administration. On the 31 March he turned his attention to the difficult decision of what to do about his brother John.

Richard and John were both sons of Henry II and Eleanor of Aquitaine. Their Kingdom was vast by medieval European standards, incorporating Normandy, Anjou, Ireland, Brittany and England. Henry had done extremely well centralising royal rule and shifting the axis of legal power from haphazard baronial justice to the Royal Courts, establishing Common Law among his people. He had made England a relatively stable place and had checked the land-grabbing inclinations of his French neighbour King Louis VII, maintaining a steady, if somewhat fractious, balance of power, a feat he also managed to replicate with the Scots and the Welsh.

Neither Richard nor John were expected to be King as their older brother (named Henry after his father) was next in line to the throne, but all the legitimate surviving male children stood to gain territory when their father died. As the eldest son and future King, Henry the younger would inherit England, Anjou and Normandy. Aquitaine would go to Richard. Ireland would go to John, leaving Brittany for the remaining brother Geoffrey.

While possessing something close to genius in administering his Kingdom and keeping external threats to his empire's security at bay, Henry failed in his personal and family life. His marriage to Eleanor was one of the elements that had at first significantly bolstered and expanded his Kingdom, acquiring Aquitaine by marriage. There was a sizeable age gap between the King and Queen. Henry was eighteen years old when they married. Eleanor was twelve years his senior. Although initially (and against expectations) the marriage was believed to be reasonably happy, it soured in time. The rift between husband and wife found its shadow in their children who allied themselves to one or the other parent. Richard was the favourite of his mother. John was the favourite of his father. The antipathy and shifting loyalties of the two sons would tear the Kingdom to pieces.

John was very much the runt of the litter. He was the youngest son and a physically small man. He was profoundly paranoid – smelling conspiracy, real or imagined, everywhere. His father, however, doted on him and would afford him gratuitous land concessions, often blind to the dangerous reaction it would inevitably provoke in his other sons.

In 1173 Eleanor orchestrated a rebellion against her husband. She set her sons against their father to counteract what she had felt were excessive land gains that the King had given to his son Henry. The rebellion was crushed and Eleanor was taken prisoner. In 1174, during the peace accord at Montmirail, the King granted his sons various land concessions and financial remunerations. John's gains proved particularly contentious as time went on. He was given numerous castles scattered throughout his eldest brother's inheritance (including Nottingham Castle). The heir to the throne was naturally resentful. But the King kept on giving land to John. In 1175 he decreed that the Earl of Cornwall's estate would revert to John when Cornwall was dead. In 1177 the King made John 'Lord of Ireland'.

In 1183 young Henry died of dysentery. Richard now stood to succeed his father as King. But his father decided, in addition to everything else he had given John, to let him have Aquitaine as well. Aquitaine had been promised to Richard. He had effectively ruled his mother's Kingdom for a decade and to have it taken away from him was an inexcusably provocative act. Six years later Richard allied himself with the French King, Phillip II, and rebelled.

Father and son went to war. The reason had been the wilful favouritism Henry had shown his youngest. Yet John's loyalty to his father was not a certainty. John's response was to wait and see which faction the war favoured and then pitch in on the winning side. The once formidable King was now old and in poor health. Richard was the more gifted soldier. Henry fared badly. John made his decision. He abandoned his father and joined Richard. The King was defeated and, shortly after his capture, he died.

Richard I was keen to put his new Kingdom in order before embarking on the adventure that was to define him as a monarch: his crusade to the Holy Land. With Richard absent

The statue of King Richard I outside the Houses of Parliament. Richard laid siege to Nottingham Castle in 1194 when his brother John rebelled against him.

there was a particular need to placate and restrain John in order to minimise the chance of an insurrection. John's allegiance to Richard in the rebellion that had ended their father's reign was no guarantee of future loyalty. Richard's response was conditional generosity. He didn't contest the lands that his father had promised John. John could have Somerset, Dorset, Cornwall and Devon, as well as Derby and Nottingham. But Richard would keep control of the castles (including Nottingham). Most importantly, Richard insisted that John could not enter England for three years. If this rankled then Richard permitted John a very generous financial incentive to behave. While most of Richard's Kingdom was being siphoned for cash to pay for the impending holy war, John was exempt, and could keep his money. Richard had also taken John's side in a dispute with the Archbishop of Canterbury over his younger brother's choice of bride, his wealthy second cousin Isabella of Gloucester.

Richard had other reasons to tread especially carefully with John. Richard was childless. He had named his heir and it wasn't John. Their brother Geoffrey had been killed in a jousting accident, leaving a widow and a young son, Arthur of Britanny. Richard chose Arthur to be his successor over John. It was a potentially volatile decision, but Richard was confident that John had been sufficiently sated with an abundance of land and money to bother trying to undermine the King in his absence. Richard went to war. As soon as Richard was safely gone, John rebelled.

In 1191, against his brother's wishes, John returned to England. John took control of the castles at Tickhill and Nottingham. A power struggle erupted in England between John, his mother, and various supporters loyal to the King. The struggle was complicated and England's loyalty waxed and waned between the sides. But John's fortunes were given a boost when it seemed that the warrior King would never return home. News had begun to trickle back to England that Richard was a prisoner, captured on his way back from the Holy Land.

Richard's famous crusade was a mixed bag of incredible success and disappointing failure. Richard took Cyprus and secured it as a strategically indispensable station for future invasions of the Holy Land. He had won a great victory at the city of Acre but failed ultimately to take Jerusalem. He acquitted himself well against the revered Muslim General Saladin, but fell foul of his own allies. Richard had gone to war with Duke Leopold of Austria and King Phillip II of France fighting alongside him. Richard's relationship with Phillip was put under strain when he reneged on his promise to marry the French King's sister in favour of a wife suggested by his mother Eleanor of Aquitaine. Richard's alliance with Leopold shattered when his soldiers trampled the Duke's colours while entering Acre. Richard compounded the insult when he refused Leopold an equal share of the plunder. The Duke had his revenge when a shipwrecked Richard was caught by Leopold's men trying to cross the Alps. Leopold gave Richard to the German Emperor Henry VI. An immense ransom was demanded for Richard's release and it looked for a while that John was safe to pursue his usurpation in relative peace. John even enlisted the help of the ever-treacherous Phillip II to gum the works for his captive brother. Phillip marched into Normandy with John's approval. John proclaimed that Richard was dead. John also sought to ally himself to Phillip by marriage (disregarding the lengths his brother had gone to approve the match with his second cousin). But Richard's release was eventually negotiated, the ransom was paid and the King of England came back.

With Richard reclining in Nottingham, the castle having fallen without too much fuss and relatively little violence, the King issued an ultimatum. John had forty days to come before his brother and surrender or else submit to the judgement of Parliament. John failed to make the journey. Richard took John's lands and disinherited him, eventually confronting his brother in Normandy. John humbled himself before the King and begged his forgiveness. Richard was merciful and restored his brother's lands. The King was believed to have said to John, 'You are a child. You have had bad companions.' John was permitted back in the country and spent time at his favourite castle, Nottingham.

None of John's brothers had died of natural causes. Richard had courted the most danger and his was always the life most likely to end in violent death. In 1199, at Chalus, the great hero of the Third Crusade died of wounds received from a crossbow bolt in an inconsequential siege over a vassal's undeclared revenue. Before Richard passed away, he stated that John was to be his heir.

John was now King and all of his legitimate brothers were dead. Left to his own devices, and without sly or powerful family members to form alliances with or hide behind, John would lose the majority of his father's holdings in Europe and turn the English, Scots and Welsh against him. But it was his dispute with the Welsh that led to the most horrific atrocity of his reign, committed on the battlements of his beloved Nottingham Castle.

From 1203 onward John spent most of his time in England. He had fallen out with Philip II who had taken much of John's land in France. Arthur of Brittany, John's nephew and former heir to the throne, had disappeared. John had had him murdered. He naturally denied it, but very few believed him. No one wanted to aid him in his wars with the French King and John was forced out of France and back into England, his lands gradually falling to Phillip II.

As far as Wales was concerned, John's beginnings were promising. He had a valuable and powerful ally in Llywelyn, the ruler of Gwynedd. The Welsh King had allied himself to John

The old gatehouse at
Nottingham Castle.

Nottingham Castle as it appears today.

through marriage to the King's illegitimate daughter Joan. Llywelyn was the ascending power in the region and was eager to maintain good relations with the English King. In 1209 he joined John in his war against the Scots. But a year previously Llywelyn had committed the cardinal error of expanding his own territory, unwittingly sowing the seeds of suspicion in his paranoid father-in-law.

Llywelyn had moved against his enemy Gwenwynwyn and taken southern Powys. John was not happy. His resentment and mistrust gnawed away at him until 1211 when he perceived that enough was enough. In his own mind his Welsh ally had grown too powerful and was now a potential threat. John decided that Llywelyn needed to have his wings clipped. He invaded Gwynedd, setting fire to Bangor, forcing Llywelyn to submit to him and recognise him as his heir. John took Llywelyn's son Gruffyd hostage and had him interned at Nottingham Castle as an insurance against any possible retaliation or future rebellion.

John may have retained the greater part of Welsh loyalty if he had stopped there: not all of the Welsh nobles were friends of Llywelyn and many were still willing to serve the King. But John embarked on a policy of castle-building and hostage-taking. Alongside Gruffyd, twenty-seven sons of Welsh Lords were imprisoned in the Midlands castle. John had succeeded in making a martyr out of Llywelyn, unifying much of the normally divided Welsh nobility against him.

The Welsh had a powerful and unexpected supporter in Pope Innocent III who had clashed with John over the appointment of the Archbishop of Canterbury. The Pope had excommunicated John in 1209 but not before imposing an interdict on his lands. The interdict meant that no one could perform a mass or baptize their child or say last rites while John remained in opposition to the Pope's wishes. The Pope's ruling was a virtual religious licence for anybody to invade or usurp the heretic King. The Pope encouraged Welsh rebellion and

King John hangs the sons of Welsh noblemen from the battlements of Nottingham Castle.

lifted the interdict for anyone who would oppose John. The King's castle in the Ystwyth Estuary was burned and attempts were made to restore Llywelyn to power.

In July 1212 news reached John of the Welsh plots against him. The *Nottingham Date Book* describes the King hunting near Clipston Palace as he received the news. He flew into a rage and called an immediate council. John sat under an oak tree and asked for consent to kill all the hostages held at Nottingham Castle. The council agreed. John vowed not to eat bread until all the hostages were dead. The King rode to Nottingham.

The twenty-eight prisoners were believed to have been playing sports within the castle walls when the order was given to have them executed. The age of the prisoners was between twelve and fourteen years old. The hostages were grabbed and bound and carried screaming to the battlements where they were hanged from the ramparts. In his anger the King had not thought for a second to differentiate between the sons of rebels and the sons of those still loyal to the throne. It is doubtful that he cared.

TWO

◇◇

The Landlocked Privateer

Edward Fenton

In the last quarter of the sixteenth century a Nottingham man served with two of England's greatest seafaring heroes, Martin Frobisher and Sir Francis Drake. He triumphed under the command of one and disgraced himself in the service of the other. Toward the end of his career he found a degree of professional redemption in the war against Spain. His name was Edward Fenton.

In October 1576 a ship sailed into an English port. Onboard the ship was a Yorkshireman, an Eskimo and a mysterious lump of black rock. Within a short amount of time the whole of London was buzzing with excitement.

The Yorkshireman was the volatile navigator and former pirate, Martin Frobisher. He had returned from a voyage of discovery commissioned to explore the virgin waters of the northern oceans. Frobisher believed he had found the 'North West Passage', a strait that was said to have linked the landmasses in the North Atlantic with the Kingdom of Cathay, where Marco Polo had first encountered the Emperor Kubla Khan. Frobisher was mistaken, but his journey was no less spectacular for that. In actuality he had sailed around the south of Greenland, erroneously believing it to be Friesland. He continued until he reached Baffin Island off the coast of Canada, thinking it to be Atlantis. *En route* a pinnace had been lost in a storm and Frobisher's ship had capsized. He had righted the small vessel by cutting the rigging loose and ordering his crew to chop

Edward Fenton.

down the mizzen mast, saving their lives in the process. Thick walls of ice prohibited Frobisher from landing on Baffin Island, but a smaller island permitted him access. Here Frobisher found the black rock that would cause so much fuss in London. He also discovered a small strait that he believed to be a rivulet that would eventually feed into the North West Passage. But extremely bad weather looked certain to hamper the exploration of the strait. Frobisher understood that he would have to turn back home or risk death.

Frobisher was painfully conscious of the fact that he had failed to achieve the main objective of his mission. He reasoned that he would need something exotic to take back with him that would distract the wealthy elite who had funded his voyage, until he could cobble together enough funding for a second expedition. The ships company had spotted an Inuit community inland and Frobisher made overtures of friendship toward them. Relations were cordial until the Inuits kidnapped five of Frobisher's men. The men were never seen again. Frobisher responded in kind. He had made efforts to win the Inuit's confidence, snatched one, and took him to England.

The possibility of a new trade route that was not controlled by the Spanish was of immense significance to the English, but any interest that might have been generated on its own terms was eclipsed by the black rock Frobisher had brought back with him. The Inuit barely lasted a week in England before dying of a cold. But the brief novelty of an Eskimo in London had bought the Yorkshireman some breathing space as rumours had begun to circulate that the black rock contained traces of gold.

Assayers tested the rock but, with the exception of a single Italian alchemist, no expert discovered any trace of the precious metal. Yet the alchemist's findings swayed the judgements of potential investors and, most decisively, the Queen herself. A second voyage was speedily commissioned.

The new fleet consisted of four ships: the Michael, the Gabriel, the Judith, and the Queen's vessel, the Aid. Captaining the Gabriel was Nottinghamshire's Edward Fenton. It was Fenton's first command and he knew virtually nothing of seafaring or the ocean.

Many of the great sea voyages of the Elizabethan age set sail from Deptford on the River Thames.

The Elizabethan era fostered an explosion of genius across the disciplines of literature, science, politics, exploration, commerce and war. It was an age of relative meritocracy, where (within reason) a lowborn individual could rise to prominence in their chosen field through sheer dint of talent. However, a rise to prominence in Elizabethan terms meant attracting the attention of a notable patron, who could subsidise and protect their charge until they had risen to a place of power and autonomy in their own right. When the system worked, the benefactor protected their protégé and was an indispensable ingredient in their attaining success in English society. But it was a precarious and fickle era in which fortunes could be reversed and favours easily withdrawn if the talented caused offence, or failed once too often.

The inverse to all of this was the sorry fact that the talentless, the average and the mediocre could advance beyond their ability because they themselves were either powerful, rich, well liked, or well connected. A man could become something he was not qualified to be simply because he was either titled, moneyed or commanded the affections of someone who was. Edward Fenton had one foot placed in either camp and over the next decade would glorify and shame himself in almost equal measure.

Edward Fenton was born in the village of Sturton-le-Steeple in Nottinghamshire. His family was rich and powerful. His brother Geoffrey would rise to a place of power in Irish politics (earning the criticism of the poet John Donne who called him 'A notorious bribe taker'). It was in Ireland that Edward Fenton made something of a reputation for himself as a soldier. His entry into the world of maritime adventure came courtesy of Ambrose Dudley, the Earl of Warwick, who was the brother of Robert Dudley, the Earl of Leicester, and favourite of the Queen. Warwick was also patron to Martin Frobisher and his influence at court had neutralised any misgivings amongst investors in the first North West Passage voyage concerning Frobisher's chequered past (which included two stints in gaol for piracy). The umbrella of Warwick's protection would have the same effect when it came to the question of Fenton's lack of experience.

Fenton's first voyage was dangerous, but not quite as eventful as Frobisher's previous expedition had been. There was less a sense of the ominous second time around as the small fleet sailed north. Although Fenton, Frobisher, and his explorers would be forever ignorant of the true geography of their destination, and would continue to make severe navigational errors, there were certain frightening allusions that they were no longer sailing under. In preparation for the first voyage, Frobisher had been schooled in navigation techniques by the famous mathematician and court astrologer Dr John Dee. Dee had advised Frobisher that once he had sailed clear of Scotland the ocean was likely to give way to an ethereal place where land, sea and air did not exist, but merged into a single substance called Thule. Frobisher now knew this not to be the case. He also knew that there was human life and gold in the north. He believed that it was only a matter of time before the North West Passage was fully explored, and that new trade routes would soon open up to the English. Yet in spite of this, the sense of trepidation and excitement Edward Fenton felt was incredible as the temperature dropped below anything he had previously known and he encountered fierce arctic storms and the immense mountains of ice that shadowed and dwarfed his vessel.

There had been more heavy investment in the second voyage and its mission was more clearly defined than the first. The orders were to find a place to mine for ore and to build a fort. When this had been achieved the *Aid* was to return to England with Frobisher on board, leaving behind a number of colonists and vessels. The colonists were ordered to take up residence in the fort, mine for ore and protect English interests in the area. They were to befriend the local Inuit population and research which times of year the ice would be at its least troublesome, with a view to safely exploring the strait and finding the North West Passage when Frobisher returned. The bulk of the colonists were to be made up of approximately one hundred convicts under the command of Edward Fenton.

The small fleet set sail in May 1577 and arrived in July at what had now become known as Frobisher's Strait. The plans for a colony were jettisoned. Frobisher had already dumped the convicts at Harwich before the voyage was effectively underway, making the expedition more or less exclusively a mining operation. The adventurers extracted nearly 200 tons of black rock before returning to England.

On his return to London, Frobisher's situation was precarious to say the least. It seemed increasingly unlikely that the black rock contained anything of value. The rock had been tested and nothing had been extracted. Frobisher brought in his own man who claimed that he had found gold. The rock was tested and retested. Out of 200 weight of black rock, 3s-worth of gold was apparently gleaned. The results were a disappointment for the majority, but others felt that a closer examination of the maths pointed toward a degree of financial redemption. If the gold to rock ratio was consistent then hundreds of tons of rock would yield fortune enough to cover the already gigantic costs of the enterprise, turn a modest profit and, more importantly, rescue the tarnished reputations of the mercantile community who had allied their names with the adventure. A third voyage was commissioned.

During the second voyage, Edward Fenton had acquitted himself well. He had done his duty and had even been a voice of reason when Frobisher had flown into a rage and threatened to hang one of his captains for failing to tip his hat to him. Despite Fenton's inexperience, his conduct had earned him a place on the third voyage as well as a promotion. His rank was now Lieutenant General and he was given captaincy of the *Judith* in the largest and last English fleet to set sail for the North West Passage. The third voyage would easily be the most dramatic and dangerous of them all.

Fenton's orders were essentially the same as before. Once they had reached their destination he would stay behind, command the colony, explore the land, establish friendly relations with the indigenous population and chronicle the fluctuations of the ice packs that blocked and endangered the straits so as to determine the best time of year to find the North West Passage.

In May 1578 a fleet of fifteen ships set sail from England, crossing the Atlantic in two weeks. Edward Fenton set foot on land an hour after Frobisher. He explored an Inuit camp that had been abandoned but for a number of white dogs. Frobisher claimed the ground for the Queen. The company left the camp and set sail to find Countess of Warwick Island, the landmass that had been earmarked as one of the best prospective mining sites during the previous voyage.

The fleet was soon enveloped in a thick, oppressive fog. Before long, neither Fenton nor his crew could see the other ships. However, through the fog the sound of drums and trumpets signalled the locations of the rest of the fleet.

The first real danger of the voyage manifested itself when the fleet was scattered by icebergs. It took weeks for them to find each other. Land was spied, but more ice blocked any attempt to put ashore. Frobisher spotted a strait and ordered the fleet to enter, believing it to be the same strait that he had discovered and explored in his previous voyages. He was badly mistaken.

What Frobisher actually saw was what we know today as the Hudson Strait. He would lead his fleet at least 200 miles off course and nearly sink them all.

Frobisher's chief pilot, Christopher Hall, was doubtful that it was safe to proceed and advised caution. Hall was either ignored or simply not heard in time by the majority of the fleet following Frobisher into the channel. After the initial drama of fog and icebergs, conditions at last seemed favourable and Frobisher saw no reason to waste time. But as the fleet sailed on, packs of ice had begun to move and quietly hemmed the English sailors in.

Before long the fleet was surrounded by icebergs. By midnight the weather had turned and a storm blew up. This was Edward Fenton's first real test. Out of the black, mountains of floating ice were heaved by wind and water into the heart of the fleet. The fleet was bisected. Gaps formed in the barriers of ice and many of the ships were able to sail to less hazardous waters and some chance of escape. Edward Fenton was cut off and encircled by walls of ice. By the early hours of the morning Fenton and the crew of the *Judith* were boxed in and contemplating the fact that they were probably going to die. There was nothing left to do but pray. A religious service of sorts was led on deck and seemed to greatly lighten the hearts of the crew. Shortly after the men had prayed, an opening in the ice wall revealed itself. Fenton sailed through the gap and led his men away from the immediate danger of the ice trap.

Over the next three weeks Edward Fenton probed the coast for a place to land. His ship became sandwiched between two icebergs which almost shattered its hull. Fenton came across the *Michael*. The *Judith* and the *Michael* pooled their resources for a contest with the elements. Icebergs lurched toward the vessels. They were countered with thick lumps of wood that

Edward Fenton's ship
is encircled by ice.

protected the hulls against the violence of the ice. When there was no wind, Fenton ordered his men to tow the Judith with rowing boats. When the men were too physically drained to carry on, Fenton ordered them to tie the ship to an iceberg, until their strength had returned and they could row once again.

Eventually the *Judith* and the *Michael* found a place to anchor a few miles from Countess of Warwick Island. Martin Frobisher arrived at the mining encampment a little after Fenton. The fleet had more or less survived and, once reunited, shrugged off the hazards of their recent adventures and got down to the business at hand, digging for gold.

Frobisher had been at his absolute best and close to his worst during his separation from Fenton. He had encountered similar and arguably greater dangers than Fenton, with more men and ships to look after. Frobisher's tendency to throw himself face first into a crisis, in tandem with his incredible ability to improvise, had saved the fleet. But once everybody had reached safer and calmer waters Frobisher's pathological refusal to take criticism estranged him from Christopher Hall. Hall had voiced what most everybody had been thinking, suggesting that their admiral was mistaken in continuing to insist that the stretch of water that had nearly killed them all was the Frobisher's Strait of previous journeys. Frobisher reacted by threatening Hall, who sailed away with three other ships in protest. Hall eventually returned to the fleet but kept a healthy stretch of ocean between himself and his commanding officer. Once on land, Frobisher turned his attention away from Hall and found reason to take issue with Fenton.

Fenton had distinguished himself with a fantastically bold proposition. The ship that was supposed to have provided the supplies for the colony Fenton was to govern was believed, at the time, to have been lost. This compromised the integrity of the colony enormously as there would not be enough vitals to last until Frobisher returned. Fenton offered to stay anyway with a reduced number of men and make do with whatever resources were available, although a reduced company would make the prospective settlement harder to defend if the put-upon Inuits decided to attack. It was an extremely brave offer. But whatever respect Fenton's proposal might have generated in the eyes of his commanding officer, it was soon forgotten in the wake of a feud that erupted between Fenton and two of his subordinates. Alexander Creake and Edward Robinson had refused to obey an order that Fenton had issued. Fenton appealed to Frobisher, but Martin Frobisher, who didn't tolerate any challenge, perceived or otherwise to his own authority, singularly failed to support his captain. The reason was probably favouritism, as Creake was known to be a friend of Frobisher. Fenton and Frobisher argued. Frobisher conceded a tribunal in which the two men received little more than a telling off, a pyrrhic victory that further undermined Fenton's authority.

Once again the colony was abandoned. Fenton's final task was to build a house and fill it with gifts for the Inuits in lieu of a fourth voyage. On 31 August 1578 the fleet returned home. One ship had sunk and forty men had died, mostly of exposure and exhaustion. Considering the dangers involved, those were highly acceptable losses. Nevertheless, a colony had yet to be established and the route to the North West Passage was still in question. Frobisher and his men had, however, managed to extract well over 1,000 tons of ore, the gold yield of which was expected to be satisfactory. It needed to be since £25,000 had been invested in the expedition.

In England the ore was thoroughly worked and, out of the 1,000-ton plus yield of black rock, no gold was found. Silver was discovered, which might have been of some consolation had the amount not been the equivalent in size of a pin head.

Of course none of this was Edward Fenton's fault, and once again he would come out of the voyage with a creditable degree of glory. But before the voyage was officially recognized as a financial disaster, and before Frobisher had begun his routine hunt for scapegoats (he would subsequently pull a knife on Fenton), there was a revealing epilogue that exposed a damaging flaw in Fenton's character that would later prove disastrous to him. As the return journey reached its conclusion Frobisher, having seemingly put aside his dispute with Fenton, handed command of his vessel over to the Nottingham man. Shortly afterwards Fenton was briefly involved in the capture of the pirate Thomas Halfpenny. This should have been an added feather in his cap, in lieu of the adulation he expected to receive once the ore had been valued. But Thomas Halfpenny escaped from Fenton's custody and it was commonly believed that Alexander Creake had helped the pirate in a continuation of his feud with Fenton on Countess of Warwick Island. And so it seemed that, without the presence of a powerful superior to support him, Fenton could not deal with dissent or command contrary men.

Fenton married Thomasina Gonson. His choice of wife was a wise one for a man intent on advancement. His new father-in-law had been Treasurer of the Navy. The marriage also provided a family connection with the powerful Hawkins dynasty who exerted a massive influence over naval policy. Fenton had done well and stood to do better as his next adventure would bring him into the orbit of the greatest of all Elizabeth's Sea Dogs, Sir Francis Drake.

In 1581 Drake was in the middle of a complicated series of negotiations to establish an alliance that would unite the French, the exiled claimant to the Portuguese throne Dom Antonio de Crato and the English in a joint venture against Spanish interests in the Azores. Edward Fenton was even being mooted as a possible Vice Admiral, but the expedition was slowly collapsing under the weight of diplomatic vacillation, cowardice and escalating costs. France, in particular, was dragging its heels. Drake was keen to act but deeply frustrated by the procrastination of the French. He suggested an alternative expedition while everyone was waiting for France to commit. Drake proposed that a small fleet, comprising three ships and a bark, could exploit an alliance that he had made during his famous circumnavigation of the globe. During his great adventure Drake had established a trade agreement with Babu, the Sultan of Turnate, in the East Indies, whereby the English would trade with the Sultan in exchange for naval support against Spanish-controlled Portuguese shipping.

As suspected, the Anglo-French alliance slowly and irretrievably came apart. But interest in Drake's more modest expedition had begun to gather momentum. However, there was a condition: Drake was prohibited from leading the expedition himself. One of the many reasons that the Azores venture had finally imploded was the fact that Phillip II of Spain had made it clear to the English Queen that any move against his Empire that directly involved Drake would be interpreted as an open declaration of war.

Martin Frobisher was put forward for the post of Drake's replacement. Despite his previous failures on many levels, Frobisher seemed a natural successor to Drake. But it soon became evident that one of the journey's key investors, the Muscovy Co. were not happy with the choice, convinced that Frobisher would use the voyage as a pretext for plundering the Spanish. Frobisher was also under suspicion of fraud at the time, which didn't help his suit any. Eventually Edward Fenton was selected as admiral of the small fleet. The fleet consisted of the ships *Edward Bonaventure*, *Elizabeth*, *Bark Francis* and the *Leicester*, which Fenton would personally command.

Drake visited Southampton to encourage his captains and left a very favourable impression on Fenton. The venture had begun well, seemingly anointed by the greatest sailor of his age, but under Fenton's command the journey was damned before it was properly underway. Drake had crewed the fleet with a liberal spread of veterans from his own voyage of circumnavigation. Drake didn't do this to undermine Fenton, but it ended up having precisely that effect. All of Drake's men were better sailors than their new admiral. This needn't have been a problem. Fenton's mentor, Martin Frobisher, had never allowed a lack of navigational expertise to undermine his ability to effectively command. Frobisher, for all his innumerable faults, could keep discipline and came alive in moments of crisis. Without Frobisher's support, Fenton struggled to command the equivalent respect amongst his men. To make matters worse, Fenton's personal success under Frobisher had made him arrogant. All the great sea captains, to a greater or lesser extent, were arrogant, but without the talent to mitigate against his own pomposity, Fenton was an accident waiting to happen.

In May 1582 Fenton left England. He had orders to sail for the Cape of Good Hope. As he approached the Cape, the weather began to turn. There was a consensus among the men that the route was too dangerous and that a better option would be to change course, sail through the Straits of Magellan and plunder Spanish interests in Peru. Fenton's most vocal critic was John Drake, Francis' cousin and one of the heroes of the voyage of circumnavigation. John Drake and his cronies brought pressure to bear on Fenton that he found increasingly difficult to resist. Fenton acquiesced to the demands of his men and launched an attack on three unsuspecting Spanish ships. The assault was botched. Two of the Spanish vessels escaped and one was sunk, sending anything of value it may have had on board to the bottom of the sea. As a consequence of this rash act of piracy, nobody in the vicinity would trade with the Englishmen.

Dissent amongst the fleet was endemic, with Fenton at one point even considering firing on his own men. Fenton could not keep his fleet together, so they separated. John Drake was shipwrecked off the River Plate. His men were picked off by Indians, or else captured by the Spanish. John Drake remained a prisoner of the Spanish for the rest of his life. He was forced to recant his Protestant religion and never saw England again.

Fenton's fleet had deserted him. He was returning home empty handed. His men hated him. His mind began to unspool. On the return journey Fenton began to insist that his crew change course and take him to the Island of St Helena, where he intended to crown himself pirate King and plunder the surrounding waterways. The plan came to nothing and Fenton returned home in disgrace, augmented by the arrival before him of his vice admiral, who had been busy dragging his name through the mud. The burgeoning realisation that Edward Fenton had been responsible for the loss of Francis Drake's cousin didn't help matters. The voyage had cost an ominous and ironic £666.

Fenton's punishment was to be banished into administration. He would stay there until open war broke out between England and Spain, when he would discover that there was work for all kinds of sailors, disgraced or otherwise.

In the years preceding the outbreak of war with Spain, Elizabeth's great old dynastic pirate and slave trader, Sir John Hawkins, now Treasurer of the Navy, was making a pre-emptive bid to ready England for the inevitable naval onslaught. English ships were radically redesigned to be more manoeuvrable than the larger Spanish galleons. English guns were also redesigned to be of a longer range, with a greater rate of fire. In 1587, Pett and Barker, the Royal Master

Francis Drake. Edward Fenton served under Drake during the disastrous Peruvian expedition that cost the Nottingham privateer his reputation.

Shipwrights, surveyed all available vessels for battle readiness. When the Spanish Armada sailed against England in 1588 all sins were forgiven and Edward Fenton was called back into service. He received a ship relative to his station and track record, the *Mary Rose*. Built in 1557, the warship was old and considered to be unsafe by Pett and Barker. It was made as seaworthy as possible and adapted to the new, but as yet not properly tested, theories of English naval warfare.

During the Armada campaign Edward Fenton took part in what came to be known as the Portland Bill Engagement, off the Dorset coast. He was sailing under the command of Lord Admiral Charles Howard. The *Mary Rose* and the *White Bear* were at the head of the fleet following Howard's vessel, the *Ark Royal*, which was in turn following Sir Francis Drake aboard the *Revenge*. It was night time. The ships were sailing in virtual blackness, as any light would alert the Armada, which was believed to be nearby. Drake navigated and hung a lantern at the stern of his ship, so that the English fleet could follow him, and that their position would not be betrayed to the Spanish. Howard's lookout aboard the *Ark Royal* saw Drake's light disappear. He didn't bother to tell his admiral, and thought nothing of it when the light reappeared, albeit a little more forward than it ought to have been. The *Ark Royal*, the *White Bear* and Fenton's *Mary Rose* followed the light. Behind them, in the dark, the rest of fleet had either stopped or slowed down.

Dawn broke and the morning sun revealed to Edward Fenton and the captains and crews of the two other vessels that what they actually had been following for most of the night was the back end of the Spanish Armada. Drake was nowhere to be seen and the light that they had thought belonged to him was in reality a lantern at the stern of a Spanish warship. Both sides were equally surprised. It transpired that during the night Drake believed that he had seen the lights of enemy ships nearby. He snuffed out his own ships lantern and went to investigate. Drake claimed later that he had neglected to inform the fleet of his intentions as he didn't want them to follow him, in case he was mistaken and had put the fleet at unnecessary risk.

Charles Howard. Fenton achieved a degree of professional redemption when he fought under Howard's command at the Portland Bill engagement during the Armada campaign of 1588.

This was of little comfort to Fenton as he almost sailed within range of the Spanish guns. Mutual surprise and superior English manoeuvrability saved Fenton and his compatriots as they quickly sailed back to the relative safety of the English fleet.

A day later, on 2 August, the Spanish Admiral Medina Sidonia launched an attack against Howard. Drake was nearby but was prevented by the wind from joining the fight. The two fleets closed in on each other. The Spanish assumed that the English intended to board their galleons, or else repulse Spanish attempts to board their own. Either way the Spanish expected the matter to be settled by bloody hand-to-hand fighting on the decks of one or the others' ships. This was how sea battles were fought and the Spanish excelled at this kind of combat. But Howard had no intention of fighting just yet. The English came dangerously close to the Spanish, as if to engage, and then manoeuvred out of their way. Fenton witnessed confusion amongst the Spanish fleet as the English slipped out of range.

Martin Frobisher, and a few other English vessels, were too inland to join Howard, and were effectively cut off from the rest of the fleet. Frobisher captained England's biggest ship, the *Triumph*. Sidonia saw an immediate chance to punish the English and sent four gigantic, heavily armed galleasses (the type of ships that had cut swathes through the Turkish fleet at the battle of Lepanto seventeen years previously) against the *Triumph* and the rest of the English stragglers. Frobisher fought back with signature fury and brilliance. He avoided shooting at the thick hulls of his enemies ships, and deliberately targeted the oarsmen of the *San Lorenzo*. As the English cannonballs hit the oars of the galleass, large splinters of wood cut through the ranks of the galley slaves, severely hampering the ability of the Spanish warship to manoeuvre properly.

Fenton may have seen his former commander going about the business of humiliating the Spanish. He probably wouldn't have seen Drake, who was waiting with much of the English fleet for the wind to favour him, so that he could join the battle and surprise Sidonia. Fenton was busy manoeuvring the *Mary Rose*, along with the rest of Howard's ships, to attack the Spanish and relieve Frobisher. The wind favoured Drake and he launched his attack. Sidonia sent the majority of his ships to tackle Drake. He turned his own galleon, the formidable *San Martin*, against Howard.

Edward Fenton was ordered, along with the rest of Howard's portion of the fleet, to sail in line, alongside the *San Martin* but just out of range of their guns. The English ships discharged their weapons into the side of the Spanish Admiral's vessel, turned around and did it again. Fenton's view of his enemy became increasingly marred by the smoke that was pouring out of both side's gun barrels, rendering targets virtually invisible. Sidonia, for his part, saw his rigging demolished and heard ball after ball thump into the side of his vessel, as the English exercised their own brand new, innovative and rarefied form of naval warfare. The *San Martin* was hit by 500 cannon balls in the space of an hour, managing to fire eighty shots in response.

The fight too'd and fro'd until both sides ran out of ammunition and the battle fizzled out. Neither side managed to sink a boat. There were very few casualties. The Spanish could not close with the English and board their ships. The English guns were not powerful enough at that range to sink or cripple their enemies. But the day technically belonged to the English, and in subsequent battles they would learn to get closer and the damage would follow.

The Armada campaign raged throughout the late summer and early autumn of 1588. English harrying tactics, and a liberal use of fire ships, scattered the Spanish along the English coast. Storms did the rest. Edward Fenton's brother witnessed over 1,000 drowned Spaniards strewn over a five-mile stretch of Irish coastland.

From the deck of the *Mary Rose*, Fenton directs fire at the Spanish Galleon, the *San Martin*.

The imposing entrance to St Nicholas' Churchyard in Deptford Green, where Edward Fenton was buried. Fenton shares his resting place with the murdered Tudor playwright Christopher Marlowe.

The Armada campaign was to be Edward Fenton's last significant naval adventure. He had failed to achieve his ambition. Fenton was only ever really piratical middle management, at his best when subordinate to strong, inspired leadership. But relative to his ability he had done well. Fenton had obeyed orders and the *Mary Rose* was praised for its part in the Portland Bill Engagement. Fenton had gone some way toward redeeming himself professionally. He went back into administration and prospered, working as deputy to Sir John Hawkins. It was the best possible end to a chaotic career.

Edward Fenton died a year after Queen Elizabeth I. He passed away in relative peace, outliving his mentors and avoiding the protracted deaths by gangrene and disease that eventually claimed the lives of Frobisher and Drake.

The Nottingham Privateer was buried in Deptford, the London heart of Elizabethan naval affairs.

THREE

Wading Through Blood

John Hutchinson and the Siege of Nottingham

In 1671 a Puritan widow wrote a detailed account of her disgraced husband's life and military service in the English Civil War. The memoir was intended solely for her children as a way of reclaiming a distinguished life that, under the retributive shadow of the Restoration, had become a byword for treason. *The Memoirs of the Life of Colonel Hutchinson* was formerly published in 1806, 115 years after its author's death. Apart from undermining many long-standing misconceptions about what constituted Puritanism, the memoir was both a moving testimony to a vibrant marriage and an often visceral account of the conflict that took place in and around Nottingham during the First Civil War.

John Hutchinson and Lucy Apsley first met in Richmond. Lucy was born in the Tower of London. Her father Sir Allen Apsley had been knighted by James I. Apsley was made Lieutenant of the Tower, and in his capacity as chief gaoler had known Sir Walter Raleigh during the Elizabethan adventurer's final internment before his execution.

Lucy was a ferociously intelligent girl. When her mother had fallen pregnant she had dreamed that a star had come down from the heavens and had touched her on the hand. This was seen as a prophetic indication of the special nature of the new child. Both parents poured money into Lucy's education. She consumed books. She mastered Latin, had a photographic ability to memorise sermons, shunned the company of other girls and, as she grew older, any man who might have felt inclined to marry her.

Colonel John Hutchinson.

John Hutchinson was born in Owthorpe Nottinghamshire, lower down the social spectrum than Lucy but still very much a part of the moneyed classes. His family legacy was bizarre, blighted by the premature deaths of elders and the incompetent or outright criminal stewardship of wayward guardians. John's grandfather had died leaving his father Thomas under the guardianship of Sir Germaine Pole who, according to Lucy Hutchinson, 'had done him so many injuries that he was fain, after he came of age, to have suits with him.' Pole's response was to try and kill Thomas Hutchinson. Pole attacked his ward as he was getting out of a boat on the Thames. Thomas defended himself by stabbing Pole in the torso with his sword. The sword broke on a metal breastplate hidden beneath Pole's coat. The bungled assassination and botched act of self-defence degenerated into an inelegant brawl that only ended when Thomas Hutchinson bit his guardian's nose off.

John Hutchinson was spared any attempts on his own life during his childhood, but was almost killed when a coach he was travelling in ran out of control. He was saved only when his nurse threw him out of the carriage and into a field just before the coach overturned.

As a youth John's education came courtesy of a string of tutors and a five-year spell at Cambridge. He was privately schooled in arms and was considered a very good swordsman.

When John Hutchinson entered the social merry-go-round of court life at Richmond, in the flurry of introductions Lucy was one of the last people he met. His future wife was currently in the middle of one of her characteristically self-imposed exiles from frivolous company. John struck up a rapport with Lucy's sister. The younger sibling's descriptions of Lucy began

The Tower of London, where John Hutchinson's remarkable wife Lucy Apsley was born.

to conjure up in Hutchinson's imagination an eccentric but captivating picture of the mystery woman. In a patriarchal culture John was fascinated by the fact that a female could have such a fluent command of Latin. He was further intrigued to find that Lucy had been the author of a particularly pleasing sonnet that he had heard read earlier during his stay. When the two eventually met, the foundations had already been laid for a profound friendship that would evolve into love and then marriage.

Lucy came down with a case of smallpox before her wedding. Distraught that her condition might leave her permanently scarred, she was convinced that John would refuse to marry a potentially disfigured bride. His response was to postpone the wedding until Lucy was better, reassuring her that he would marry her regardless of the condition of the scarring. Lucy recovered from the illness. Her face was mercifully unmarked. The couple wed and in 1641, after three years in the South of England, moved to Nottinghamshire.

Back at home John Hutchinson, who had always been intellectually and morally inclined toward a Puritan point of view, subjected his own beliefs to a rigorous self examination. He underwent something of a spiritual awakening in the process and became utterly convinced of the primacy of the Puritan interpretation of Christianity. Yet Hutchinson was far from dour. He was famous for having resplendent long hair, in contrast to the more favoured severe crop that would later give rise to the name 'Roundhead'. He also enjoyed music and was more favourably disposed to the arts than most Puritans of his era. He had a theological integrity that would put him at odds with his brethren if he felt that they were honouring tradition over Biblical precedent. Where principle was concerned, John Hutchinson took little account of consequences and would very rarely back down.

A portrait of Lucy Hutchinson.
(Courtesy of Nottingham City Council and www.picturethepast.org.uk)

Hutchinson's moral refortification could not have come at a more useful time as the country was about to be immersed in violent civil conflict. What had begun as a dispute between the King and his parliament over taxation had escalated into a multitude of pretexts for war that cut to the centre of people's spiritual beliefs and challenged the very notion of the King's divine right to do as he pleased.

John Hutchinson tried to objectively weigh the evidence as to which side he would fight for. His allegiance was to Parliament. But Hutchinson was slow to war and prayed to God that a peaceful resolution might be reached. Although potentially a capable soldier and a boon to whichever side he chose, Hutchinson's induction into the conflict would be almost accidental.

In 1642 Royalist soldiers had begun to gather in the Midlands. King Charles I would soon raise his standard at Nottingham, officially beginning the war against Parliament. Sir John Digby, the High Sheriff of Nottingham, attempted to take the town's supply of gunpowder. John Hutchinson opposed him. Although provocative, Hutchinson's actions were not intended as a declaration of loyalty to Parliament. His concern was principally for the safety of Nottingham, believing that no army had the right to deprive a town of the ability to defend itself. A further dispute with a Royalist quartermaster who tried to billet a General in his house ensured that Hutchinson was marked as a Puritan troublemaker. A warrant was issued for his arrest and Hutchinson was force to flee Nottingham until the presence of a Parliamentarian army in Northampton forced the King to withdraw to Shrewsbury where Royalist support was more certain.

With the King's army gone, prominent Midlands' towns made efforts to secure themselves for their various chosen sides. John Gell raised a regiment and fortified Derby for Parliament.

Charles I begins the Civil War just outside Nottingham Castle. The area was subsequently named Standard Hill to commemorate the act. (Courtesy of Nottingham City Council and www.picturethepast.co.uk)

Standard Hill as it appears today.

ON A MOUND ABOUT 30 YARDS
TO THE REAR OF THIS TABLET
CHARLES I
RAISED HIS STANDARD
AUGUST 25TH 1642.

The plaque on Standard Hill that marks the start of the English Civil War.

This was a mixed blessing for the cause as, according to Lucy Hutchinson, Gell's troops 'were good stout fighting men', but, 'ungovernable wretches' and Gell himself was 'a foul adulterer.' Royalists tried to take Nottingham for the King but were beaten to the town's weapons cache by Nottingham's Parliamentary contingent. Nottingham formed a Defence Committee of influential local men. Colonel Francis Pierrepont made John Hutchinson a lieutenant colonel. Newark declared for the King and became the East Midland's principle stronghold for Royalist opposition.

Although none of the great battles of the English Civil War were fought in Nottinghamshire, the county was of great strategic value to both sides. Being centrally placed in the country, whoever controlled Nottingham effectively controlled troop movements from the South to the North. For the Parliamentarians, the loss of Nottinghamshire meant that their armies in the North would be cut off from supplies and support from London. It seemed imperative to each side to monopolise the county. Consequently the first significant military action in the region was an attempt to storm Newark and take it for Parliament.

The coalition of Nottingham, Derby and Lincoln forces botched the assault. Their failure was echoed around the country as Parliament floundered in the early stages of the war. The King's wife Henrietta Maria had arrived in the north of England from Holland with reinforcements. She had marched south and was expected to attack Nottingham *en route*. Roundhead reinforcements were sent from London to meet the threat. Among them was Oliver Cromwell who expressed a liking for John Hutchinson's 'plainness and openheartedness.' The Queen's forces engaged in a standoff with Parliament. But apart from sporadic canon fire, the expected battle did not happened. The Queen's army sidestepped Nottingham and marched on.

On 29 June 1643 John Hutchinson was given charge of Nottingham Castle. The castle was a disgrace. It was a virtual ruin, barely habitable and, as it stood, practically indefensible. Its supply of food and powder was worryingly low. What made matters worse was the fact that the fresh injection of troops were needed elsewhere. Sir John Meldrum, the Commander of Forces for the Nottingham District, took the best of the Horse and Foot to raise a siege in Gainsborough. This left Nottingham's defences stretched extremely thin. Hutchinson reasoned that he could not defend the town and hold the castle at the same time. He stripped the town's defensive works of their canon and moved them into the castle grounds. Many of the Aldermen of Nottingham were furious and threatened mutiny. Hutchinson was forced to make arrests and send the prisoners to Derby. He called a meeting to explain to the people of Nottingham the realities of their town's position as he saw it. With a frank disregard for diplomacy he said, 'you have but three ways to choose: either leave the town and secure yourself in some other Parliamentary garrison; or enlist into the castle; or stand on the works and have your throats cut.'

Nottingham responded in mixed fashion. Some stayed and some left. The castle was strengthened with an influx of men who, provided they could help with repairs by making their quarters habitable, were welcome. Hutchinson sent his wife and children away. Many defenders sent their families to the surrounding villages. Extra powder and match arrived from London and Hutchinson's small force raced to make the castle as defensible as it could possibly be before the inevitable Royalist attack.

A Cavalier envoy representing the forces of the Duke of Newcastle came to Hutchinson and formally demanded the surrender of Nottingham Castle. According to military etiquette,

Hutchinson entertained his enemy within the castle walls. Courtesy was repaid with ridicule. But George Hutchinson, John's brother, replied: 'If my Lord must have that castle he must wade to it in blood'.

The envoy left and the castle defenders readied themselves for an attack they were barley prepared for. Hutchinson delivered a surprisingly frank speech to his men warning them that if they saw their houses on fire from the castle parapets then they were to accept the fact and even be prepared to torch their homes themselves if it served the common good. He told them to expect 'hard duty, fierce assault, poor and sparing diet, perhaps famine and want of all comfortable accommodation.' He went on to tell his men that they were all probably going to die but that they must determine to fight to the death rather than surrender the castle to their enemies.

Once again the assault failed to happen as Newcastle's forces were diverted to attack Hull instead. Hutchinson used the reprieve to concentrate on strengthening the castle. During this time Hutchinson's father had died. Military duty meant that John Hutchinson was unable to tend to the vacant estate which was plundered by bands of Royalists. This type of behaviour was not solely the province of the enemy. Gell's Derbyshire Roundheads were equally prone to pillaging. But Hutchinson made every effort to try and curb this impulse in his own men, insisting that they pay for what they took when patrolling the countryside.

Lucy Hutchinson returned to her husband in the castle and would be present for the next bloody episode in the contest for Nottingham.

Direct threats had little effect on John Hutchinson. His enemies resorted to bribery and emotional blackmail. The Governor of Newark entreated John to surrender for his family's sake and offered to return extorted rents taken from his father's estate if he would change sides. John refused the offer.

On 18 September 1643, 600 Royalist troops from Newark were given entry to Nottingham by a treacherous Alderman. Nobody in the town bothered to alert the castle. Many of Hutchinson's men had defied orders to stay in the fortress and had snuck home to sleep in their own beds, leaving only eighty defenders within the castle walls, most of whom were asleep. As Hutchinson's men opened the castle gates the following morning they were fired on by Royalist soldiers. The castle gates were quickly closed denying the enemy entry. The Royalists sent soldiers up the tower of St Nicholas' Church and fired into the castle grounds. The sniping killed one old man and kept Hutchinson's soldiers pinned down until night, when under the cover of darkness he ordered a trench dug that ensured that his men could pass between the castle gates without getting shot when the sun rose the following morning.

With Hutchinson boxed in, the Royalists plundered Nottingham. They built a fort on Trent Bridge and placed prisoners in pig pens in the town market place. Hutchinson responded by directing canon fire from the castle with grisly results. Intelligence reached him that five Royalists commanders were gathered at a certain house in the market place. A canon ball hit the house, beheading an old lady who was in the act of receiving payment for information given to the Royalists.

Hutchinson's force was doubled when eighty of his men managed to sneak back in to the castle. The siege was lifted when reinforcements from Derby, Leicester and Lincoln cleared the streets of Royalists. The Royalists held their position at Trent Bridge. But John Gell's Derby men, having dislodged the enemy, then proceeded to plundered the town.

A Royalist soldier uses the roof of St Nicholas' Church to shoot into the grounds of Nottingham Castle.

St Nicholas' Church. Hutchinson tore down the original church building when Royalist soldiers used it as platform from which to shoot into Nottingham Castle.

Throughout the five or so days of the conflict Lucy Hutchinson, in the absence of a surgeon, had been dressing the wounds of the injured in the castle.

An initial attempt to take the stockade at Trent Bridge failed. Hutchinson ordered the demolition of St Nicholas' Church and redoubled efforts to take the fort. A bloody assault was anticipated but the Royalist had abandoned their position. Hutchinson put his brother in charge of the fort.

A thanksgiving service was given to praise God for a bloodless victory at the river. John Hutchinson refortified the castle and the fort. The castle began to manufacture its own powder and cast its own mortars. Hutchinson was granted the authority to raise his own regiment of 1,200 men and was made Governor of Nottingham Town and Castle, a promotion that caused envy among the Defence Committee who would prove a more insidious threat to his authority than a host of Cavaliers.

With the exception of a moment when the Duke of Newcastle's army camped once again outside Nottingham and looked like they might give battle this time, combat in the following months was limited to the odd raid or skirmish. There were internal squabbles with the Defence Committee but Hutchinson managed to maintain charge of the town.

On 15 January 1644 rumours that Royalist forces in Newark were marching on Sleaford reached Hutchinson. It was a campaign of misinformation designed to make Hutchinson lower his guard. The Royalists were on the move but Nottingham was their target. Hutchinson saw the ruse for what it was and prepared the town and the castle for attack. With a fresh influx of men and weapons

St Nicholas' Church, viewed from the battlements of Nottingham Castle.

Hutchinson had rearmed and manned the defensive works around the town. On 16 January, 3,000 Royalist soldiers were spotted marching across the countryside toward Nottingham. Hutchinson sent the Foot to reinforce the Horse at the town's defensive works. Both Foot and Horse panicked at the sight of the approaching army and ran back to the castle. The Royalists walked into Nottingham uncontested and sent soldiers up into the church tower of St Peter's and began to fire into the castle.

Hutchinson was incensed at his own men's cowardice and ordered them back into the streets to battle for Nottingham. The fighting was ferocious. The Royalist force heavily outnumbered Hutchinson's men but the Roundhead's were fresh to the fight. The Cavalier's energy had been sapped by the winter march and the debilitating wet of dampened clothes. The Royalists were scattered into the surrounding countryside, a map of their retreat painted in splashes and trails of blood.

A month later the enemy were back but in a more covert fashion this time. A group of soldiers dressed as townsmen (some of them in drag) with numerous pistols, clubs and hatchets hidden about their person tried to get into Nottingham. Hutchinson's spies once again did their job and the raid was intercepted. Fighting on the bridge pitched a number of the raiders into the Trent, four of whom drowned.

St Peter's Church was also used as sniping platform by the Cavalier forces during the numerous attempts to take the castle during the Civil War.

Over the next few months the balance of power ebbed and flowed across the East Midlands. Another attempt to take Newark failed. The King's nephew and soldier extraordinaire Prince Rupert came within a hair's breadth of burning Nottingham to the ground but was called south before he could make good on his intentions. Colonel Thonhaugh, one of Hutchinson's most able allies, was wounded in the arm and stomach and was laid up in bed as a consequence. During all this time the internal opposition against Hutchinson intensified. Throughout the campaign Hutchinson had endured criticism for moving the town's guns into the castle as well as disciplining one of his own men for mistreating prisoners. Against his conscience pressure from the religious authorities obliged Hutchinson to arrest some of his own men for unorthodox worship practices. He later released them. Their incarceration was deemed too short and Hutchinson added the local clergy to his increasingly long list of foes. Hutchison's enemies attempted to turn the convalescing Thornhaugh against him, trying to convince the wounded colonel that Hutchinson was usurping his authority when he had taken temporary command of Thornhaugh's soldiers while the colonel was recuperating from his injuries. It got to the point where a significant number of Hutchinson's own men were refusing to carry out his orders if directly contradicted by the Committee. Hutchinson was forced to leave his command and take up the issue with Parliament in London.

Hutchinson was obliged to travel to the capital twice before the question of who was the final authority in Nottingham concerning matters of warfare was properly resolved. Parliament decided in Hutchinson's favour. In his absence a sermon was preached against him, various Committee members absconded with money reserved to pay the town's soldiers and the Trent fort fell once again to the enemy, leaving a butcher's bill of twenty dead Parliamentarians. When Hutchinson came home he retook the fort and received the closest he had ever come to a hero's welcome.

Oliver Crowell was on the ascendancy. He had engineered a powerful victory at Marston Moor and was reorganising the rag-tag semi-professional soldiers who had typified the conflict up to that point into the formidable New Model Army. Cromwell was tipping the balance of the war in Parliament's favour. The Roundheads won another crucial victory at Naseby. Leicester fell to Parliament. The war was being won. In the autumn of 1645 much of the King's now beleaguered army had regrouped at Newark and all available Parliamentary forces in the area were needed for the siege that was to follow.

Hutchinson had been ordered to help destroy the Royalist garrisons around Newark. He must have felt a degree of relief committing to a stand up fight with an unambiguous enemy that he could see and kill. Under the command of Major General Poyntz, Hutchinson entered the town of Shelford with his men. He was almost immediately subjected to the now obligatory sniping from a church rooftop. He ordered the church to be burned and the men smoked out. There were only a few marksmen to contend with. The majority of the enemy were holed up at the heavily defended Governor's Residence.

For once none of Hutchinson's men ran off or skulked away when the shooting started. They fought together. Attackers were buffeted from their ladders by large logs thrown from the walls of the Governor's Residence (Hutchinson himself being twice knocked from a ladder). His mounted soldiers joined the Foot and the walls were cleared. Hutchinson and his men entered the grounds of the house. They were shot at from the windows and for a while were trapped in the yard. Hutchinson should have been wearing armour but had chosen to wear a thick buff coat instead. He engaged in hand-to-hand duel with a Cavalier captain and killed him. The death of the captain unnerved his followers and they backed off. Aware of Hutchinson's position, Major General Poyntz was attempting to force his way in to relive his subordinate. He shouted out to Hutchinson calling to him by his rank. This was a mistake as the cowed defenders fighting spirit was suddenly reinvigorated when they realised that the buff-coated swordsman was a high-ranking Roundhead and redoubled their efforts to attack him. Hutchinson was saved by the brave intervention of his brother George.

Eventually the Governor's house fell to Parliament. Poyntz was for killing all the prisoners. Hutchinson interceded and their lives were spared. The Governor was found wounded and naked on a manure pile. Hutchinson gave him his coat. The Governor died a day later. During the night the house was burned down.

Hutchinson served out the remainder of the First Civil War in the siege of Newark. When King Charles eventually ordered Newark to surrender, Hutchinson entered the town to find it despoiled and ravaged by the plague.

For the time being the war was over. When it flared up again in 1648 Nottingham was virtually untouched. Hutchinson's fighting career was at an end. He was made MP for Nottinghamshire in the Long Parliament and the governorship of the castle passed on. Hutchinson's last act was to secure a payment of £5,000 to the men that had fought under him but had been robbed of wages by their own Defence Committee. John Hutchinson returned to Owthorpe with his wife. His house was a mess and his finances in disarray as he had spent much of his own money in the defence of Nottingham when funds were short coming. He was also a sick man and for the next four years suffered from severe pains in his head which according to his wife 'bought him near to the grave.'

Hutchinson took part in the trial of King Charles and was one of the many signatories on the Sovereign's death warrant. The King was executed, his heir was banished and England became a Republic.

This was perhaps the bitterest pill of all for Hutchinson, for over the course of the next few years he observed Cromwell consolidate his power, establish what looked to Hutchinson and his wife to be a dynastic line, and transform himself into the type of tyrant that Hutchinson had

Colonel Hutchinson killed a Royalist captain in hand-to-hand combat during the fight to take Shelford.

Oliver Cromwell. Cromwell expressed admiration for Hutchinson during the war but despaired at his decision to pull down Nottingham Castle.

sacrificed his health and fortune to dispose of. Hutchinson foresaw future conflict and could not stand to see his town subject to more fighting and divisive bloodshed. Nottingham's military currency lay in the defensibility of its castle. Without a castle Nottingham was strategically irrelevant. While Cromwell was in Scotland, John Hutchinson ordered Nottingham Castle to be destroyed.

Cromwell's death and the Restoration of the monarchy complicated Hutchinson's life further. On his return, the new King Charles II had many of the regicides put to death and desecrated the corpses of those that were already dead and buried. But Hutchinson was spared when, without his consent, his wife forged his signature and wrote a letter making a persuasive case for clemency. It would prove to be only a stay of execution.

In the mid-1660s forty-four people were arrested in connection with a suspected rebellion in the North. Twenty-six were condemned to death. Two of them were spared. The rest were killed and their heads mounted on poles. From the standpoint of the reinstated monarchy the rebellion provided the perfect excuse to deal with all the perceived Republican ringleaders who had escaped the earlier regicide cull. John Hutchinson was arrested in Owthorpe and sent to the Tower of London. He was transferred to Sundown Castle in Kent. His beloved wife Lucy and their eldest daughter moved south to be near him. The dilapidated conditions of his new prison degraded his health. On 11 September 1664 John Hutchinson died of illness before he could suffer the indignity of a show trial and execution.

FOUR

'A proud and conceited Frenchman'

Marshall Tallard and his Comfortable Prison

From 1705, for over half a decade, Nottingham became one of the most picturesque prisoner of war camps in the British Isles. Blenheim, the first great battle of the War of Spanish Succession, had been fought. Despite superior numbers and a strong defensive position the French and their Bavarian allies had lost. Their defeat had been total and humiliating. Many captured high-ranking soldiers were brought to England. Eleven were sent to Nottingham, its landlocked, geographically central position discouraging any notions of escape.

The architect of Franco-Bavarian military destruction was the up-and-coming soldier-savant John Churchill, the First Duke of Marlborough. Leading a Confederate army of central European principalities, strengthened by crack English soldiers, Marlborough's victory was aided in no small way by the questionable actions of his opponent Camille d'Houston, the Comte de Tallard, Marshall of France and the most prominent of all the prisoners of war sent to Nottingham.

Before war had broken out Tallard had already spent a considerable amount of time in England. A favourite of Louis XIV, Tallard was known for his wit, excellent taste, erudition and intelligent grasp of European affairs. He was well liked but not especially trusted. As a soldier he had taken part in the War of the League of Augsburg achieving the rank of Lieutenant General, but his real expertise lay in diplomacy. In 1698 he was made French ambassador to the court of the English King, William III. It was a crucial time in European politics. Carlos II of Spain was dying and had no direct heir to succeed him. Great pains had been taken to ensure that Carlos' replacement would look after the interests of the surrounding European powers, avoiding the sort of power monopoly that might result in warfare. The First Partition Treaty had been drafted naming Joseph Ferdinand, the Arch Duke of Bavaria, as Carlos' successor. The treaty granted, amongst other things, French land gains as well as trading rights for England and Holland.

The unexpected death of Joseph Ferdinand threw a spanner in the works. The treaty was now void. Tallard was engaged in the redrafting of a second treaty but events were rapidly running ahead of themselves. In 1700 Carlos II died. His will named the French King's grandson Phillip of Anjou heir to the Spanish throne. Political and diplomatic etiquette still required delicate negotiation to carve up Spanish interest among Europe's elite if the fragile balance of power was to be maintained and war averted.

Marshall Tallard.

In 1701 Louis XIV sent troops into the Spanish Netherlands to occupy twenty fortresses that were now technically his grandson's property. It was undoubtedly perceived as an act of aggression as far as the Dutch were concerned. In the same year James II, the exiled Stewart King of England, also died. Louis declared James' son the rightful heir to the English throne. It was either a wilfully naive or deliberately inflammatory action. English trade with Spain was being disrupted. Fighting between Austrian and French troops had broken out on Italian soil. It was a difficult year for Tallard whose constant reassurances to the English that France wanted nothing but peace were rendered hollow by the provocative actions of his monarch. The English recalled their ambassador from France. Tallard was expelled from the country and returned home. On 15 May 1702 England declared war of France. Yet France was in a seemingly unassailable position. Their army was one of the biggest in Europe and its reputation was formidable.

William III died and Queen Anne took his place. Marlborough was placed in charge of her forces and sent to Europe.

The relative strength or weakness of Austria would be the key to the war's initial success. Maximilian Emanuel II von Wittelsbach, the Elector of Bavaria (and son-in-law to Leopold I of Austria) had thrown in with the French and provided them with a power base by which they could consolidate their forces and march on Vienna. The early stages of the war would stand or fall on who could either secure or dislodge the Elector.

On returning to France Tallard's political ascendancy had been put on hold and he had been given a military command. Tallard won an early and notable victory at Speyerbach and was instrumental in taking the town of Landau. He received the Marshall's Baton. Shortly afterward, through an ingenious campaign of misdirection, Tallard managed to distract his Austrian foes sufficiently enough to take an army of 35,000 men under their noses through the Black Forest and deliver it to the Elector of Bavaria and his French compatriot Marshal Marsin, without losing a single man. In the early stages of the war Tallard had shown great initiative and innovation. He looked like he would flower into a gifted commander and seemed an ideal opponent to set against the as yet untested English General on his way to do battle with the French and Bavarian forces.

Marlborough was on the move but his intentions were a mystery, his enemies unsure as to where he was going to attack. In May 1704 Marlborough entered hostile territory.

He conducted a series of false manoeuvres along the Danube that convinced the French that he was at various points going to attack either Phillipsburg, Alscace, or Landau. The French dispatched troops to intercept him, and wherever they went they found that he had gone somewhere else. On 7 June, Marlborough eventually revealed his hand and marched straight into Germany. The French were in the wrong place and Marlborough took his men through a gap of his own creation, unimpeded by the vast army opposing him. On 10 June he met up with his allies, the Margrave of Baden and Eugene Prince of Savoy.

The French High Command scratched their heads for a while trying to figure out what Marlborough intended to do. They hedged their bets and split their force. Tallard was ordered back across the Black Forest Mountains with more soldiers. He was instructed once again to reinforce Marsin and the Elector but stay with them this time and take command in anticipation of a possible clash with the enemy. The march was less textbook second time around. Many of Tallard's horses became sick and his cavalry were weakened as a consequence. He was also shadowed for a while by Eugene of Savoy but the prince and his army vanished almost as quickly as they had appeared.

Marsin and the Elector had fared badly. The Confederates had attacked them at the fortress of the Schellenberg and had taken it. Marlborough's soldiers were torching the Elector's villages and the Elector had weakened Marsin's force by sending his own men to protect his endangered property. The arrival of Tallard on 5 August could not have come at a better time. Despite the setbacks Tallard was confident of victory. Their army was thought bigger and was definitely more experienced. Although bamboozled by Marlborough's impressive sleight of hand at the Danube, his presence so far inside enemy territory seemed ridiculous. Warfare was seasonal and it was already August. It was unlikely that the English Duke would risk a pitched battle with the French. Victory was unlikely. Allied supply lines (a key to any invading army's success) had to be strained. The invading Confederate force would need to do whatever it was they were planning to do soon or winter would ruin their chances of any kind of success and the gains that they had made would be lost.

On 10 August the Franco-Bavarian army crossed over to the north bank of the River Danube. News reached them that Savoy and Marlborough had reunited and that their forces were nearby. Marsin, the Elector and Tallard all agreed that the Confederates had over extended themselves and were preparing for a tactical retreat. The Elector and Marsin were for attacking the enemy's rear sooner rather than later. Tallard said no on the grounds that it made little sense to be hasty when time was their ally. When the Elector's troops had been recalled from his estates Tallard would sanction an attack, when their own army was at its strongest.

On 12 August the Franco-Bavarians chose the ground from which they intended to launch their campaign. It was a good defensible position. The army was laid out on the plains of Hochstadt. To their front were three villages that could be easily garrisoned. To the right was the Danube. To the left were mountains. Any army foolish enough to attack them frontally would have to cross the stream of the Nebel and trudge through marsh land to get to them. Tallard placed his own forces on the right. Marsin and the Elector were positioned on the left. At Tallard's disposal were roughly 140 squadrons of cavalry and seventy squadrons of infantry, a little fewer than 60,000 men. The very notion of a direct assault was outlandish.

On 13 August at six o'clock in the morning a sleeping Franco-Bavarian army woke up to observe the combined forces of the Confederate Alliance marching toward them, seemingly in an attacking formation. Some officers were alarmed. Many dismissed the sight as a retreating enemy puffing out its chest as it was forced to conduct a humiliating and dangerous withdrawal. It took a full hour for the reality of the situation to dawn on Tallard who had been asleep in the village of Blenheim. Even when confronted with the advancing army Tallard was so convinced he was watching a retreat that he had even dispatched a letter to his beloved King Louis telling him as much.

By seven o'clock it had become obvious that the Confederates actually intended to attack them. Tallard called a war council. Opinion was sharply divided as to what to do next. All three commanders agreed that the Confederate forces probably outnumbered them, that Marlborough and Savoy and the Margrave of Baden were all present. No other conclusion justified the confidence to assault such a well defended position. Marsin and the Elector wanted to check the enemy at the marsh, gun them down and repel them as they tried to cross the difficult and boggy ground. Tallard rejected their plan. He wanted to demolish the whole army and not simply drive them back. He proposed the notion of letting the entire enemy force cross the Nebel and then meeting them head on with his cavalry. The infantry stationed in the villages of Blenheim and Oberglau would assault the enemy flanks with musket fire and then finish them off with bayonets. Marsin and the Elector advised against what they perceived to be a reckless plan. They had had the advantage of fighting these soldiers at the Schellenberg and had been stunned by their enemies' ferocity and discipline. Tallard's response was dismissive and contained an implicit accusation of cowardice. He said, 'I see today the victory will be my own.'

The initial stages of the battle went well. A brigade approached Blenheim. Tallard's cannon slaughtered many of them and killed still more as they crossed the Nebel. At one o'clock, after enduring a bloody three hour bombardment of artillery, Blenhiem was eventually assaulted. The English were thrown back and their colours taken. Hessian soldiers retrieved the colours. English and Hessian troops attacked Blenhiem again pressing the fight to the outer streets of the village. Someone inside Blenheim called for reinforcements. Tallard's reserves on the right flank poured into the village. But Tallard failed to check them and the village filled to bursting with 12,000 soldiers. The streets of Blenheim were now dangerously overcrowded. The defenders could not move. The attackers broke off their attempt to take the village and seemed content simply to shoot into the streets confident that even the most poorly aimed shot would wound or kill somebody. Over the course of the day the chaos became so great in Blenheim and the congestion so total that some of the defenders managed to set themselves on fire and were burned to death.

As they crossed the Nebel and marched across the plain, five squadrons of Confederate infantry were charged by eight squadrons of French cavalry. The French horsemen were intercepted by five squadrons of English cavalry. The English cut the French to pieces and drove them from the field. In spite of the sickness that currently blighted many of their mounts, Tallard's cavalry were still considered the elite shock troops of Europe and it was unthinkable that a numerically inferior force could do what Tallard had just seen them do to his best soldiers. Ostensibly the engagement was a glorified skirmish, but in reality it was a key moment in the battle. Tallard was deeply traumatised by what he had observed. His confidence began to disintegrate and it is questionable whether he made a coherent military decision from that point onward.

Elsewhere on the battlefield Prince Eugene's forces were being violently repelled as they tried to attack Marsin and the Elector on the left. In the centre Marlborough's force had crossed the Nebel virtually unchallenged. Tallard ordered a cavalry charge. It was an uncoordinated assault but worried the attacking army nevertheless.

A crisis erupted to the left of Marlborough's centre. A combined surprise assault by infantry and Marsin's cavalry had managed to shoot and cut its way through Danish and Hanoverian attackers and looked as if it might be about to do the same to forces commanded by the Confederate Prince of Holstein Beck. The Prince requested help from a Habsberg ally but was refused. The Prince was taken prisoner. A gap was being forced and for while the Confederate centre looked in serious danger of total collapse.

At this point Marlborough personally took charge of the situation. He ordered three reserve battalions and artillery to make haste across the marsh and plug the gap. He requested reinforcements from Eugene of Savoy who gave them without question despite being under murderous fire from the defenders on Tallard's left. The French cavalry were driven back to the village of Oberglau and the centre was restored.

By mid-afternoon the battle was raging on a four-mile front. Marlborough succeeded in getting the bulk of his army into the centre where he could now deploy his cavalry. This was the one area where he knew he was stronger than Tallard. Marlborough had more horse than Tallard did, many of which had been deliberately held back from the fight until this precise moment. The full audacity of Marlborough's genius was about to become painfully apparent to his enemies. Marlborough had never intended to take Blenheim or Oberglau, or turn the right or left flank for that matter. His strategy from the beginning had been to contain the left and the right and convince his enemies that he had far more men than he actually did. In truth Eugene of Savoy was fighting a defending force numerically superior to his own, and the Margrave of Baden and his army weren't even present at the battle. It was all smoke and mirrors until Marlborough decided that it wasn't. Tallard had more guns and infantry than his opponent but less cavalry. Marlborough understood this and had forced Tallard to fight the most decisive part of the battle where the English Duke was at his most powerful and dangerous.

Between three and four o'clock there was a respite in the fighting as the two armies seemingly caught their breath in anticipation of the last exchange. The final clash of cavalry looked evenly matched for a while. But the coordination of Confederate horse with infantry platoon fire drove Tallard's cavalry back. The defeat of Tallard's horse left his supporting infantry completely isolated. It was shot ragged and much of it finished off with point blank canon fire. Tallard requested reinforcements from Marsin who, oblivious to what was going on in the centre, refused him. The Franco-Bavarian centre broke and the rout of their army began, many hundreds of soldiers drowning in the Danube as they tried to get away.

In all, including the dead, the wounded and those taken prisoner, the Franco-Bavarians suffered 40,000 casualties, two thirds of their entire force.

Tallard was captured by Hessian cavalry. He had been wounded in the hand. During the battle his son had been injured and would later die of his wounds. Marsin and the Elector of Bavaria managed to escape.

Marlborough treated the captured Marshall with a high degree of courtesy, permitting Tallard the use of his coach. Marlborough rightly deduced that Tallard would be pilloried for the loss

After his defeat and capture at Blenheim, Tallard was shipped to England. He was put ashore at Greenwich and taken to Nottingham.

Newdigate House, where Tallard served his time as a prisoner of war in relative luxury.

of an entire French army and allowed the fallen Marshall to write his own account of the battle to the French King. A subordinate of Tallard delivered the dispatch to Louis on agreement that he returned to Marlborough and resumed his captivity once he had fulfilled his obligation. Tallard was taken back to England and imprisoned in Nottingham.

'Imprisoned' was a relative term. Because of his rank and station Tallard was effectively on parole. He lived in Newdigate House on Castle Gate. He paid a rent of 50s a week, and so long as he did not try to escape, had the run of the town. He was an avid and creative gardener. Tallard loved food and local legend has it that his servants scoured the countryside looking for wild celery, a vegetable not greatly used in the cooking pots of Nottingham prior to Tallard's arrival and widely believed to have been introduced to the county by the French soldier.

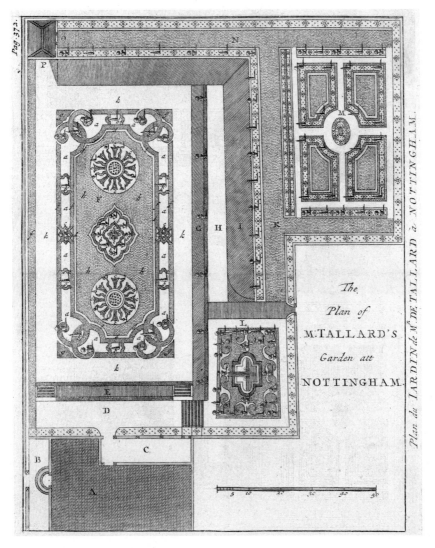

Tallard's design for the garden at Newdigate House. (Courtesy of Nottingham City Council and www.picturethepast.org.uk)

Nottingham lads fight each other for the amusement of Tallard and his fellow prisoners of war.

Tallard was generally well liked in Nottingham and, if the novelist Daniel Defoe is to be believed, repaid like for like with the town's women folk leaving a biological bequest of small Marshalls behind him. The man that Blenheim veteran and diarist Captain Robert Parker had once called 'a proud and conceited Frenchman' was known locally as 'the great man at Nottingham'.

Peace agreed with Tallard more than warfare ever did. But his time in Nottingham did leave one odd martial legacy. Another local legend has it that Tallard and some of his military cronies would pay local boys to box and wrestle in the town market place. Tallard was impressed with their ability to give and receive punishment. He praised their courage and declared Nottingham lads amongst the bravest he had ever seen.

Tallard was released in 1712 and received back into the French court by Louis XIV who, despite the widespread national ridicule to which his protégé had been subject, never publicly criticised him.

FIVE

◇◇

'Damn the trade'

Nottingham and the Luddites

On Sunday 10 November 1811 Mr Hollingworth, a Bullwell hosier, sat in his home with seven or eight armed men making ready for a siege. The object of the anticipated assault were six frame knitting machines that Hollingworth had had removed from his workshops and brought to his home. That evening a large of group men arrived at the house and tried to force their way in. Both sides had firearms. Both sides opened fire and exchanged shots for a while. The attackers entered the house and attempted to smash their way into the frame room. John Westley, the first man through the door, was shot in the stomach. He died within moments of being hit, but tried to rally his men on with his last few breaths. The attackers broke off and left with the corpse of their fallen comrade, which they took to the edge of the Forest. It was a misleading reprieve. With the body temporarily interred, the attackers came back to finish what they had started. Hollingworth's guards had had enough and abandoned their employer. The gang entered the house and smashed the hosier's frames to pieces.

Throughout the week similar attacks were visited on hosiers around the Nottingham area. Seven or eight frames were burnt in Basford. A thousand men (300 of whom were armed with guns) purged Sutton-in-Ashfield of frames, destroying fifty-six. The authorities managed to make a few arrests and four men were taken to the County Gaol. But the army was too thinly spread around Nottinghamshire's villages to do much good.

The military was present in full force during John Westley's funeral. Westley was originally from Leicester but had lived in Arnold for twelve years where his burial was to take place. There was anything between 700 and 1,000 mourners present. The funeral procession had been dogged by a mixture of magistrates, mounted soldiers and constables under the command of the High Sheriff. A drum was beaten by the soldiers that interrupted the church service. The authorities read the Riot Act. They permitted the body to be placed into the ground and then had the graveyard cleared.

Earlier that year there had been wave of frame-breaking riots throughout March. The riots had caused so much consternation among the authorities that two police magistrates had been sent from London, as well as soldiers from the North, to support them. Riots *per se* were nothing new to Nottingham, but November's violence was different in character and consequently more disturbing for the authorities. This was not a mob. The men who had smashed Hollingworth's frames were more akin to a guerrilla army. They were incredibly

John Westley is killed as he leads a Luddite attack on the house of a Bullwell hosier.

well armed and disciplined. Their organisation was controlled and impenetrable. Their targets were carefully chosen: their use of violence was precise and discriminate. They had a profound understanding of terror but were generally approved of by the populace. They were the Luddites.

Master Hosiers were the new enemy. They had incurred the hatred of the mob and the Luddites because of unforgivable compromises they had made to one of Nottingham's principle economic mainstays, the lace trade. Lace makers were highly skilled workers who made quality products either in their own homes or small workshops. They were answerable to the Master Hosiers who rented them the knitting frames on which they did their work. It was an industry vulnerable to exploitation. The master hosiers could (and did) raise rents on machines and lower wages at will without serious interference. But in the late eighteenth century hosiers introduced two hugely divisive practices that effectively created the Luddite movement. These practices were 'cut ups' and 'colting'. Cut ups were mass-produced cheap lace items. With a new type of kitting frame little skill was required to manufacture goods quickly and sell them at competitive prices. It made a degree of economic sense but the reduction in quality was appalling. To the untrained eye the difference was imperceptible but cut up lace was prone to come apart at the seams very easily. Colting was the practice of employing frame operators who had not served proper apprenticeships and were consequently far less skilled than the traditional lace manufacturers. Both practices marginalized legitimate craftsmen to the point of poverty. Cut ups and colting, more than anything else, provoked the trade to violence.

Nationally the government was taking measures against suspected radical infiltration of industry. Fear of revolution born out of the wars with France gave birth in 1799 to the Combination Act. The change in the law effectively made anything that resembled a union illegal. This legislation further weakened the position of the lace workers and fortified their employers. By 1811 the lace trade was ready to respond. It was a twofold retaliation, both lawful and unlawful, giving birth to the Nottingham Framework Knitters Association and the Luddites.

The association was technically illegal under the Combination Act as it was a *de facto* union but no one seemed keen to press the point and they were allowed to operate. The association's leader was an intelligent self-educated man named Graverner Henson who sought to bring the hosiers to account via the machinery of Parliament.

The Luddites aims were exactly the same as the Framework Knitters Association. They despised the use of cut ups and the practice of colting, but were not interested in the rule of law. They singled out merchants who endorsed these hated practices. They would post a warning of their intentions to their proposed target, giving them the opportunity to amend. If the warning was ignored then the Luddites would arrive at their house during the night. The Luddites would be disguised, wearing a mask or a handkerchief across their face, or else be blacked up. They would come armed with a mixture of guns, axes, swords or hammers. One Luddite would command the rest and be referred to as Captain or General Ludd. Lookouts were posted while the rest of the men went into the house or workshop and smashed the frames to bits. When the attack was over the Luddites regrouped outside and a roll was called, each Luddite having been assigned a number beforehand. Finally a pistol was fired into the air and the Luddites would disperse.

A masked Luddite.

The Luddites were a highly secretive organization. Members were believed to have taken oaths. To breach the oath could mean death. Luddites were fiercely loyal and virtually impossible to infiltrate. Spies consistently failed to penetrate their ranks. The hefty rewards posted for information leading to arrests were largely ignored. No Luddite literature exists and no former Luddite ever chronicled the workings of the organisation. The identity of their pseudonymous leader Ned Ludd was never revealed (although many suspected he was actually Graverner Henson). Although clearly a frightening organization, fear of retaliation only accounts for some of Nottinghamshire's reluctance to take against the Luddites. In truth the Luddites were very popular. They were not perceived as thugs and at this stage in the conflict were extremely controlled in their use of violence. The Luddites also took financial responsibility for honest lace workers who had been compromised by their attacks and often compensated them.

The authorities' response to Luddism was varied and desperate and would become increasingly tough as the conflict escalated. Because the Luddites entered homes to carry out their attacks, the incursions were deliberately interpreted as burglary, which carried the death sentence. As Luddite attacks continued into the winter months of 1811, curfews were imposed on public houses which were required to shut up shop at ten o'clock at night. More troops were siphoned into Nottingham and the Prince Regent established a £50 reward for any information leading to the conviction of a Luddite.

The conflict continued into 1812. The sophistication and forward planning of the Luddites became formidable as they managed to smash eight frames in Carter Gate without being heard, evade troops across the Trent and fox an armed hosier by disguising themselves as soldiers. But criminal elements were beginning to use Luddite activity as a pretext to plunder. To begin with, the Luddites were quick to punish those who acted in their name but breached their code of ethics. A group of looters caught by Luddites outside Clifton only narrowly avoided being lynched because of the nearby presence of soldiers. But a new commitment to brutality seemed to typify the Luddite movement in the New Year. In one attack a woman was hit over the head with a pistol to stop her screaming, and worse was to come.

A Luddite gunman attempts to assassinate William Trencham, after the Hosier ignored warnings to pay his servant girls a decent living wage.

The ante was upped considerably when a bill was put forward in Parliament to make frame-breaking punishable by death. The bill was considered an outrage by many (including a significant number of hosiers), the Luddites' most famous advocate being Lord Byron who delivered a stinging rebuke to the government in the House of Lords. His words carried little weight and the bill became law in February. It was a month that also saw the introduction of the Nottingham Peace Act, which gave magistrates the power to appoint more constables. The idea was to have an increase of constables patrolling the streets day and night. The Act was essentially a police draft. Refusal to answer the call would result in a fine. The law was created with Nottingham in mind but had a universal application. Yet it was not particularly enforced in the town it was intended to benefit.

Some headway, however, was made against the Luddites. March saw nine suspected members of the movement put on trial. Two were acquitted whilst seven were sentenced to transportation. Significantly, none of them were hanged. The Luddite response came a month later.

William Trencham, a local hosier, had received a letter on behalf of Captain Ludd damning him for paying women in his employ scandalously low wages. Ludd was incensed to discover that 'these unfortunate girls are under strong temptations to turn prostitute from their extreme poverty'. In retaliation, Trencham was rumored to have fined two of his employees and provoked the Luddites further by daring them to tell Captain Ludd exactly what he had done. Returning from a party in Market Street, Trencham was shot outside his house on Kayes Walk. Two men had been waiting for him hidden behind a tombstone. They opened fire with a horse pistol.

Kayes Walk, where hosier William Trencham was shot by Luddites.

An assassin's-eye view of Kayes Walk. Armed Luddites hid behind a gravestone as they waited for William Trencham to return home.

The bullet hit Trencham in the chest. He survived the attack and a 100-guineas reward was posted for information leading to the arrest of the assailants; 500 guineas would be granted if the arrest led to a conviction. Nobody claimed the reward. In spite of the disturbing shift in terms of violence, the Luddites still seemed to retain public support.

The attempted assassination of Trencham couldn't have come at a worse time for Graverner Henson and the Framework Knitters Association. The association's intention had been to draft a bill that would bring the abuses of the Master Hosiers to Parliament's attention and legally stamp out the practice of cut ups and colting. Henson was trying to drum up support from Leicester, Glasgow, Devon and Tewkesbury in lieu of an attempt to convince Parliament of the justice of the lace maker's cause. He tried to muster support from his Irish equivalents, but had no success. In 1812 he put together a petition to Parliament and in April submitted the bill to the House of Commons. Henson planned to present examples of well made and cut up lace. He also intended to present witnesses to Parliament. But trying to unify his allies had been an exasperating process. Henson was frustrated that his compatriots weren't sending sufficient funds to cover his witnesses' expenses and that they were dragging their heels submitting examples of Nottingham lace to London. His frustrations were evident in a letter he sent back to Nottingham denouncing his own with the words, 'Damn the trade, they seem determined on their own destruction.'

In July, having been watered down by Parliament, the bill was eventually rejected in the House of Lords.

The intensity of Luddite violence in Nottingham began to diminish just at the point when it had started to flare up in the North of England. On 27 April William Horsfall, an outspoken and unpopular opponent of Luddism, was murdered in West Riding. On the one hand, the failure of the Association of Framework Knitters increased support for the seemingly more successful tactics of the Luddites. But Horsfall's killing was in many ways the beginning of the end for the Luddites. For the faithful, this new act of violence calcified their resolve to do whatever it took to further their aims. To the nominal, who might otherwise have supported the Luddites, the murder scared and horrified them enough for their support to be gradually withdrawn over the coming months and years. But there was still enough hatred of the establishment to perpetuate the Luddites for a little while longer. This depth of ill feeling was no better demonstrated than in the public reaction to the assassination of Prime Minister Spencer Percival, who was shot dead in May by John Bellingham. The assassin was cheered by the crowd when he went to the gallows, and in Nottingham news of Percivals's death was met with public rejoicing, much to the disgust of the authorities.

For the next five years there were sporadic resurgences of Luddite activity but the line between political violence and gangsterism was becoming increasingly blurred. On 9 June 1816, William Wright of New Radford was visited by Luddites. In time-honoured fashion

The Shire Hall. Luddite Daniel Diggle was hanged in front of the Shire Hall for his part in the shooting of a Radford Hosier. (Courtesy of Thoroton Society of Nottinghamshire and www.picturethepast.org.uk)

High Pavement and the old Shire Hall building as they appear today.

his frames were smashed, but the attackers made off with yards of net as well. Two men were arrested. The authorities gave serious thought to holding the trial in Lincoln for fear that the judge and the jury might be murdered.

The cause had become polluted. Murder, theft and jury intimidation were now considered acceptable tactics. But the internal codes of honour and loyalty that had bound the organization together in the beginning, rendering it impenetrable, were also beginning to unglue. The case of Daniel Diggle typified this perfectly.

On 22 December 1816 Daniel Diggle and four other men entered the Radford home of a Mr Kerry with the intention of smashing his frames. Kerry fought back and in the scuffle a gun went off wounding him in the head. The gang left Kerry believing him to be dead.

Daniel Diggle was out again on 2 January 1817, poaching this time with a group of friends, including William Burton who had been present during the attack on Kerry. The men were poaching on the estate of Lord Middleton and took it upon themselves to terrorize his game keeper, William Shortwood. They approached Shortwood's house and fired at him through his bedroom window. The gang were arrested for the crimes that they had committed on Middleton's estate, but once they were in custody they quickly began to inform on one other. During the flurry of confessions William Burton told his captors about the attack on Kerry's house. He informed them that Daniel Diggle had been present and was the gunman that had shot Mr Kerry. Diggle was charged and put on trial.

Daniel Diggle initially pleaded guilty to the shooting but the Judge advised him to withdraw his plea. It made no difference. Diggle was found guilty and on 2 April 1817 was hanged on the steps of the Shire Hall. Diggle's execution effectively slammed the lid on Nottingham Luddism and the sequence of events that led him to the gallows demonstrated just how infected the Luddite cause had become.

SIX

The Demon of Anarchy and Crime

The Fourth Duke of Newcastle and the Mob

In 1822 Henry Pelham Fiennes Pelham Clinton, the fourth Duke of Newcastle-under-Lyne, wrote a candid account in his diary of the death of his eldest child. Later that year his wife also died while she was giving birth. Newcastle lost two more children before the year was finished. He documented his private grief in a journal. It is a moving account that provides a deeply human portrait of a man in severe emotional crisis. It is impossible not to sympathise with Newcastle. This is worth mentioning because, to the public at large, Newcastle was one of the most hated political figures in the country whose loathing was amplified in Nottinghamshire during the 1820s and '30s. In an age of radical politics Newcastle's name was synonymous with reactionary and underhand electoral practices. His intractable views would provoke the Nottingham mob to commit their most notorious act of destruction.

Newcastle inherited his title from his brother who had died within a year of inheriting it from his father. Along with the title, Newcastle also inherited Clumber Hall and its estates, as well as Nottingham Castle, now no longer a fortress but more a stately home and generally unused during the Duke's lifetime.

Newcastle was an Etonian who had done poorly at school. He had spent time in France as a youth and had returned home with a loathing of the country. He was an Anglican whose Protestantism was defined principally

The fourth Duke of Newcastle-under-Lyne.

Clumber Hall, the ancestral home of the controversial fourth Duke of Newcastle. (Courtesy of Nottingham County Council and www.picturethepast.org.uk)

The Clumber Hall site today. The hall itself has long since gone but the family church remains.

by a mistrust bordering on hatred of Catholicism. Most of all Newcastle was an old fashioned Lord of the manor in an era where the old class certainties were being openly challenged. The arena where these irreconcilable differences were being thrashed out was the municipal or general elections.

At this point in history voting was the legal province of the moneyed classes. The poor were not allowed to vote. The ruling classes didn't want them to vote, believing very strongly that the gentry's high-born position gave them a right to make all the important, moral and political decisions for any tenants under their care. A further outworking of this ethos was that many landowners believed that they had a mandate to tell their tenants who were eligible to vote precisely who to for vote for (often having chosen the candidates themselves). Failure to comply with a Duke or Lord's wishes might result in eviction. This practice was called 'boroughmongering'. Newcastle was an unrepentant boroughmonger, believing that his blood and his title gave him the right to act and think on behalf of those that God had put under his care.

Newcastle was naturally at odds with his age. The early to mid-nineteenth century was reaping the whirlwind of the radical politics that had erupted amongst the labouring classes in the previous generations. What had once been the province of marginalised visionaries, mad poets and political philosophers was now moving into the political mainstream.

The reform lobby was gaining sympathy in Parliament, and as time progressed the opponents of electoral reform were beginning to look and sound increasingly anachronistic. In 1830 the Duke of Wellington's government collapsed. Wellington was a Tory and was an enemy of reform. His replacement as Prime Minister was the Whig politician Earl Grey. The absolute priority of Grey's government was to push forward a reform bill that would overhaul the antiquated and prejudicial voting system. Grey wanted to grant voting rights to all males who owned property of £10 or more. He wanted to reduce the number of MPs in boroughs that had a disproportionate number of Members of Parliament per head of population and give the seats to boroughs that were not represented in Parliament at all despite large populations. The disparity was severe. There were boroughs of over 10,000 people who had no advocate in parliament at all, while poorly populated areas were often oversubscribed.

Up until this point Newcastle had been a patron of sympathetic candidates (usually relatives) that he would personally select and put forward. Generally it suited Newcastle to stay in the

The Duke of Wellington, the most famous opponent of the Reform Bill.

background but the government's treacherous capitulation regarding reform demanded a more public response from the affronted Duke. Newcastle began to take a more active part in parliamentary debates, publicly joining the argument in the crucial years 1829-32.

The year of 1829 began with an act of recrimination: Newcastle evicted thirty-six tenants who had failed to vote for his candidate in a recent bi-election. He was criticised in print and was still being criticised a year later when excrement was delivered to his home in an envelope. There was a written message in the envelope but Newcastle declined to read it. Just before Christmas, Newcastle had become embroiled in a dispute with the Attorney General who had publicly criticised boroughmongers. Newcastle went to London to complain in person to the Prime Minister and deliver a speech in the House of Lords defending his position.

The Duke of Newcastle began 1831 with charity. He gave to the poor as an act of seasonal benevolence, despite the fact that someone had tried to burn down one of his barns over the festive period. He genuinely believed he was a good Christian and any charitable donation to the needy on his estate was born out of an authentic sense of religious duty. He abhorred bribery but saw nothing immoral in the practice of boroughmongering. He ruthlessly dispossessed tenants who had the temerity to cross him politically but played the martyr when he was criticised by his peers for doing so. He believed that he was acting for the good and that any opposition was the penalty any righteous man could expect to receive for doing what was right.

Whatever Newcastle might have been, he was certainly not a coward. In January the Duke had been invited to a ball at Lincoln. He had also been threatened with death should he dare to turn up. Newcastle ignored the threats and travelled to Lincoln by coach. He was stopped by a horseman who warned him that a mob was waylaying carriages looking for him. The horseman said that a friend of his had already been harassed by ill wishers who had mistaken him for the Duke. The horseman implored Newcastle to turn back. The Duke seriously considered whether to carry on or go home. He decided to press on. A mob of fifty or sixty men were waiting for him in Lincoln. A constable and servants escorted Newcastle through the hostile crowd. The Duke was jostled and wax was thrown at him but he reached the ball unharmed. One of his servants however had been struck on the head. Newcastle enjoyed the ball and exalted in the fact that the mob had failed to intimidate him.

On 1 March 1831 Lord John Russell presented the Reform Bill to Parliament. The bill was met with a mixture of derision from the Tories and incredulity from many Whigs. The bill was to be debated before a second reading and then the house would vote. The debates succeeded in publicising the bill outside of Parliament and public support for the bill began to grow. Ambivalent MPs soon began to feel the pressure from their constituents. In the Midlands the Duke of Newcastle's support began to melt away, leaving him feeling increasingly isolated but nonetheless defiant.

On 23 March the House of Commons divided and the Reform Bill was passed by one vote. Tory strategy was to dilute the bill by trying to push forward a series of amendments. Grey's response was to pressure the King to dissolve Parliament before the Tories whittled the bill down to nothing. There was a moment of pure political farce as the King dashed across London to dissolve Parliament while the anti-reformer Lord Wharncliffe delivered a speech denouncing dissolution, which soon degenerated into a public slanging match, backed up with threats of violence which the King could clearly hear as he readied himself to enter the House.

On 22 April Parliament was dissolved. Crowds in London stoned the home of the Duke of Wellington and jostled the Queen's carriage. Wellington's servants drove the crowd away by shooting over their heads with blunderbuss fire.

The advantage of having Parliament dissolved was that Grey could now call a general election with reform as the driving issue, hopefully increasing the reform majority. The election galvanised Newcastle to organise candidates in the most important political contest he would ever be involved in. In Newark tensions erupted into violence and Newcastle expressed private fears that he and his own would lose.

The election was a resounding success for the reformers. Newcastle lost Newark and considered doubling the rents of his tenants as punishment for their disloyalty. In June the Reform Bill was reintroduced into Parliament. In total 267 voted against, and 367 in its favour. In July, as the bill entered the committee stage, the Tories pedantically picked over every detail, but on 22 September the bill was passed in the House of Commons. The Tories had one last powerful line of defence. The anti-reform contingent in the House of Lords was strong and irresolute. When the bill went to the Lords it was rejected by forty-one votes. The Duke of Wellington's house was attacked for a second time (a stone thrown through his window nearly hit him in the head). This was unpleasant but hardly surprising. A degree of aggravation was to be expected. But any sense of jubilation amongst the ultra conservatives was short lived as news began to filter back to London of appalling explosions of violence erupting around the country.

Newcastle was in the capital during this period. On 11 October, while attending a debate at the House of Lords, the Duke was told that Nottingham Castle, his ancestral home, had been destroyed by the mob.

News of the Reform Bill's rejection had reached Nottingham on 8 October, while the annual Goose Fair was in progress. The mayor organised a public meeting for the following day.

Apsley House, the London home of the Duke of Wellington, was surrounded and stoned during the Reform Bill disturbances.

Rioters attack Nottingham Castle.

It was supposed to be a peaceful meeting. On Sunday hundreds gathered outside the White Lion Hotel. The first smatterings of violence manifested themselves in broken glass. A druggist's windows were smashed and a doctor was attacked. Both men were suspected opponents of the Reform Bill. Come night time brickbats were being freely thrown. The mayor appealed for peace but was assaulted. The Riot Act was read. Constables and mounted soldiers tried to control the crowd but were largely ineffective.

On Monday, after a quiet morning, the mob resumed their work. They tried to destroy a mill in the Forest. They went to Sneinton and armed themselves with railings that they had prized from Notintone Place. The mob marched on Colwick Hall, the residence of an anti-reform magistrate. They looted the property and tried unsuccessfully to burn it down.

Nottingham was bereft of many of its soldiers who had been sent to Derby to deal with trouble that had erupted there. To compensate, special constables had been sworn in *en masse* during the afternoon. The representatives of law and order were stretched thin and did remarkably well for a while. The constables saved numerous properties. Magistrates, and such soldiers as were left in town, checked the mob's advance on the House of Correction. But nobody successfully opposed the 600 rioters who made their way to the castle, extinguishing gaslights as they marched. The mob couldn't smash their way through the castle lodge gate

Nottingham Castle in flames.

but three men got into the grounds through a broken panel and opened the gates from the inside. The mob started with the railings, ripping them up. They reached the castle and forced their way in. One hundred and fifty rioters entered the building. They tore tapestries to pieces and smashed statues, banisters and chandeliers. Eventually they began to set the castle on fire using furniture as kindling. By nine o'clock at night the blazing castle was visible to much of Nottingham. A large crowd watched the fire. They cheered as the lead roof melted and the castle was consumed.

The castle had apparently been unoccupied when the mob burned it down, but the following morning the bodies of two children were found in the ruins of the building. *The Nottingham Date Book* called the blaze, 'A tremendous sacrifice to the demon of anarchy and crime.'

The Duke of Newcastle knew that Nottingham Castle had been targeted precisely because it had belonged to him. He was concerned that the mob would do the same to Clumber Hall. Newcastle made immediate plans to go home. He wanted to set off straight away but it was raining too heavily to travel. He slept in his clothes and left London at four o'clock in the morning. Newcastle arrived at his estate on 13 October. He met an evacuated family who warned him that there was a danger that he might be shot by men waiting for him in the woods. Newcastle arrived safely at Clumber Hall to find his home filled with soldiers readying the property for a siege. He learned that one of his barns had been burned down and a cow had been roasted alive. Apart from that, no other violence had been done to his home or the surrounding estate.

As Nottingham took stock of the damage that it had done to itself, Newcastle was busy calling magistrates to account for negligence and loudly expressing his belief that England was on the brink of revolution. Arrests were made and in December Newcastle became aware that a Special Commission had been formed to try the offenders at Nottingham. Newcastle was incensed that his name was not on the commission. He wrote to the King who ignored him. He wrote to the influential and potentially sympathetic Lord Melbourne who replied, but only to gently instruct Newcastle that his presence on a commission trying men accused of destroying his property might be interpreted as slightly prejudicial.

In early January 1832, two judges were escorted into Nottingham by an immense guard of mounted gentlemen. London police officers were sent to Nottingham to ensure that there was no trouble. On Friday 6 January the trials of those arrested for rioting during the Reform Bill disturbances began. Only two men were charged with burning down Nottingham Castle and both were acquitted. A handful of men received the death sentence. Four had their punishment commuted to transportation. That left five men who were to be hanged. It was an unpopular decision. In the weeks leading up to their executions an escape attempt was foiled. Twenty-five thousand signatures were collected and presented to the King. Newcastle had even been approached by the relatives of the condemned and asked if he would sign their petition.

On his return from London, Newcastle was warned that rioters were waiting to kill him in the woods of his own estate.

The steps leading up to Nottingham Castle, which was burned to the ground by Reform Bill rioters in 1831.

He expressed a surprising degree of sympathy but still refused to help them, stating that he was not allowed to interfere. A day before the hangings two of the condemned were reprieved, leaving three to die publicly on the steps of the Shire Hall.

On 4 June 1832 the Reform Bill was passed and became law.

Newcastle was predictably outraged. He wrote in his diary, 'We have been betrayed, cajoled, tricked and deserted in the most basest and most shameless manner.'

SEVEN

Five Murderers

Nottingham and the Razor

In 1815 a nineteen-year-old farm worker stood trial for murder. John Hemstock had entered the property of a Mr Wells, his former employer, intending to rob him. He came upon Wells' nephew John Snell. Hemstock hit Snell with a piece of wood and cut his throat with a razor.

Hemstock was arrested, put on trial, found guilty of murder and was sentenced to hang. The Justice decreed that once Hemstock was dead his body would be handed over to surgeons for dissection. Hemstock had been reasonably composed throughout his trial but broke down when the sentence was passed. He begged the Justice to allow him to be properly buried. The Justice refused.

John Hemstock was hanged. His body was cut down and taken to the General Hospital where it was dissected and examined. Hemstock's skeleton was suspended on wires and then on put on display. The Hemstock case was Nottingham's first razor murder of the new century.

In 1844 William Saville killed his wife and children with a cutthroat razor and left their bodies in Colwick Woods.

A cut-throat razor, the favourite weapon of the Victorian murderer.

In the interim before Saville's atrocity, Nottingham's murders had been committed, in the main, with knives, bludgeons and bare hands. The Saville murders had been premeditated. He had even placed the razor in his dead wife's hands to look as if she had killed her children before taking her own life.

As the century wore on the razor appeared time and again in murders throughout the country. But unlike the deliberate character of Saville's appalling crime, Nottingham's razor killings were more often than not spontaneous explosions of violence stoked by unchecked tempers, jealousies and unrequited lusts.

In 1878 John Brooks was hanged for the murder of his lover Caroline Woodhead. When Brooks met Woodhead she was a married woman, estranged from her husband. Brooks and Woodhead lived together and their life was reasonably exotic by the standards of the time. They moved around the country, living in Lincoln and then Manchester. They travelled across the continent, settling in Calais for a season. Eventually they returned to Nottingham.

In late 1877 the couple had an argument. The dispute was serious enough to warrant Caroline moving in with her mother. On 11 December 1877 John Brooks arrived at Caroline's new home in Lenton. Caroline's mother was out. The estranged couple began to quarrel once again. In the heat of the moment Brooks pulled out a razor and slashed his lover's throat.

Brooks had committed the crime in haste and sought to get rid of the body in a similar spirit of hurry and confusion. He carried or dragged his lover's corpse out of the house and tried

The site of the Park Hospital where the murderer John Hemstock's skeleton was displayed for many years after his hanging.

After cutting his estranged lover's throat, Thomas Chollerton tried to kill himself.

to hide it at the bottom of the garden under a hedge. The body was badly hidden and quickly discovered. John Brooks surrendered himself to the police and stood trial for murder. He was hanged on 13 February at the House of Correction by William Marwood.

Later that year Thomas Chollerton, a forty-one-year-old fish hawker, killed his lover with a razor. Chollerton's lover Jane Smith had left him that May, citing poor treatment as her reason. Smith went to stay with friends at Notintone Street in Sneinton. A month later Chollerton arrived on her doorstep. At seven o'clock in the evening he entered the house. At ten o'clock screams were heard. An old man was passing by. He found Chollerton engaged in the act of cutting his lover's throat. The old man pulled him away. The police arrived. Chollerton tried to cut his own throat with the murder weapon. The police prized the razor from his fingers. He begged the police to let him be.

Jane Smith died of her injuries and Thomas Cholleton was tried for her murder. He was found guilty and hanged by William Marwood.

In 1881 Thomas Brown killed his lover Elizabeth Calderwell with a razor during a drunken argument. Brown struck Calderwell's neck with such force as to almost completely cut her head from her body. He was arrested, tried and convicted of murder. He was sentenced to hang. William Marwood was his executioner.

EIGHT

'War is cruelty'

Henry Smith and the War Between the States

On 15 March 1865 a Nottingham-born man won America's highest military accolade fighting for the North in the American Civil War. He served under two of the most gifted and controversial Generals of the conflict. His military service saw him participate in one of the most horrific battles in American history as well as one of its most contentious and divisive campaigns.

Henry Smith was born in Nottingham on 4 May 1840. His father died when he was a child. Henry was seven years old when his mother decided to leave England with her children. The Smiths settled in Canada for a while and then moved across the border to America. They tried their hand at farming and proved successful, moving to Iowa and buying their own farm in 1854.

In 1861 Henry was living at Shell Rock Falls when a handful of southern states rejected federal rule and broke away from the Union. Civil war erupted. Henry Smith was barely twenty-one years old.

Iowa elected to support the Union and called for volunteers. Henry Smith enlisted in the 7th Iowa Infantry on 8 July 1861. His initial rank was first corporal. Henry was mustered on 24 July. In August he marched with the rest of the 7th to Burlington in blistering heat. He marched on to Jefferson Barracks and then finally to St Louis where he received his service weapon, a Springfield musket. Once he had been armed he travelled by train and foot to Ironton where he was drilled and taught how to fight.

Captain Henry Smith of the 7th Iowa Infantry.

Smith was promoted to fifth sergeant on 19 September 1861. It was a rapid promotion that would seem to indicate great promise and aptitude. But neither Smith nor the rest of the 7th had yet seen combat. In November Henry Smith experienced action for the first time under the command of Ulysses S. Grant.

Grant was a courageous veteran of the Mexican-American War. He was also a drinker and possible depressive. He had left the army and tried his hand at civilian life, floundering at whatever he turned his attention to. With a long history of failure in business behind him the war would become his professional salvation as he re-enlisted and was given the rank of colonel. Abraham Lincoln had appointed him Brigadier General by the time Henry Smith served under him.

The 7th Iowa had been sent to the border between Missouri and Kentucky, two states divided by the Mississippi River. The South had occupied and fortified the town of Columbus on the Kentucky side of the water. Grant wanted desperately to fight and was keen to see Columbus taken. But as a General, he was relatively untested at this point in his career.

He had charge of 20,000 men who were believed to be disciplined soldiers but were untried on the battlefield. In November Grant took personal command of 3,000 men including the 7th Iowa. Henry Smith was among them. Grant's intentions seemed to be to provoke a fight with the enemy. He hated inactivity in his soldiers and believed that frequent combat was essential to keeping discipline and raising morale. Grant had no orders to engage, but his men were keen to attack and he was perhaps even more eager to encourage them. On 6 November 1861 Grant moved his men down river six miles away from Columbus. At two o'clock, on the morning of the 7th, Grant received intelligence that Confederate troops were crossing the river in preparation for a possible attack. Grant was in no position to assault Columbus but opposite the town was a Confederate encampment at Belmont. Grant decided to attack Belmont. In Grant's own words the plan was to 'Push down river, land on the Mississippi side, capture Belmont, break up the camp and return', thus discouraging future Confederate incursions from Columbus.

Smith and the 7th travelled across the great river in smoke-stacked steamers, waiting throughout the night in the dormant boats on Lucas Bend, and then disembarking onto the marshy ground and marching quietly through the woodland to Belmont as the dawn approached. Grant had taken a regiment down river as a rearguard in case of surprise attack. Smith was with the main force that prepared itself for the assault on the Confederate camp.

Grant sent skirmishers ahead of the main body of troops. The Confederates spotted them and the battle began. The two forces clashed.

Ulysses S. Grant.

There was an intense two-hour exchange of fire. Grant's horse was killed underneath him. The Confederates' resolve broke and they fled. In terms of their debut on the battlefield, Grant's pronouncement on his own men was double-edged. He said, 'the officers and men engaged at Belmont were then under fire for the first time. Veterans could not have behaved themselves better than they did up to the point of entering the camp.' Once Grant's men had beaten the Confederates back and entered the camp they should have pressed their attack home and taken prisoners. But the temptation of an empty camp was too much to resist and the Union soldiers set about looting the vacant tents. It is unlikely that Henry Smith took part in the looting. He had been badly wounded in the initial assault. A bullet had torn through his chest. His collar bone had also been broken.

Grant's men were now being shelled by artillery from Columbus. Grant ordered the camp torched. But his men were beginning to panic as the Confederates that they had initially displaced had regrouped and had surrounded Grant and his soldiers, cutting them off from their boats. The soldiers at the boats had failed to notice their compatriots were being encircled. They had been distracted by enemy steamers full of Confederate reinforcements that were crossing the river and, oblivious to their own men's predicament, were trying to sink the Confederate boats with captured artillery.

Grant was surrounded but unphased by the situation. His officers failed to share his confidence until he explained to them that, 'We had cut our way in and would cut our way out just as well.' The Confederates were driven from the field a second time and the battle became a race for the Union forces to reach their boats before they were intercepted by the 5,000 Confederate reinforcements who were now ashore. Henry Smith was carried toward the boats with the rest of the wounded.

Grant's rearguard had abandoned him. Grant personally rode out to hunt for enemy soldiers on a fresh horse. He steered his mount through a large cornfield, the crop high enough to obscure the General and his horse from view. He came within fifty yards of the enemy.

Henry Smith is shot in the shoulder during the Battle of Belmont.

As Smith lay wounded in a steamboat his compatriots waited for their General to return. Assuming he was conscious Smith would have heard shooting from the trees as Confederate soldiers tried to get in their last shots at the retreating Federal army. He would have heard the blast of his own army's gunboats as they returned fire. It is unlikely he would have seen his commanding officer riding up a plank and into a boat, the last free Union soldier to leave the field.

The battle was inconclusive. The losses were roughly equal, each side having suffered around 500-600 casualties including the captured, the wounded and the dead. Many regarded Belmont as a loss for Grant. But Grant retrospectively observed that the Confederates never 'detached from Columbus again.' Henry Smith was sent to the Mound City Hospital in Illinois. He healed, recuperated and rejoined his regiment.

Henry Smith had experienced battle; he had suffered, survived and regained his strength sufficiently enough to fight again. His hard won veteran status would put him in the minority of experienced soldiers who were to take part at the Battle of Shiloh.

Shiloh was, up to that point, the bloodiest battle in American history. Later in the war there would be battles that dwarfed Shiloh in terms of the numbers of casualties, but few that equalled it in its nightmarish and grotesque character.

In March 1862 the Union Army were gathering once again on the banks of the Mississippi. Their destination was the Missouri-Tennessee border. They were preparing to push south. The Union Army's strength was 40,000 and, with more men expected to arrive, their state of mind was confident, relaxed and cavalier to the point of negligence. They believed that the Confederates had no fight in them. It was a point of view shared and fostered by their Generals, Ulysses S. Grant and William Tecumseh Sherman. The Confederates were in fact mobile and an army of equivalent size was moving undetected toward Corinth, frighteningly close to the Union lines. In the two days preceding the battle both Grant and Sherman made errors that

The 7th Iowa capture a rebel canon during the Battle of Shiloh.

would cost them in blood. Grant neglected to entrench his soldiers and Sherman failed to listen to his colonels who believed that they had heard enemy activity to the south.

Henry Smith and the 7th Iowa had been at rest in Donaldson for four weeks before boarding a steamer that took them to the Pittsburg Landing. Smith had to wait a further week on a crowded ship before being allowed on shore. It was raining and there were storms. Smith set down near the river and the 7th Iowa waited, not doing very much and not much being expected of them.

On 6 April 1862 Henry Smith would have been standing to attention awaiting inspection with the rest of the 7th when news broke that a large force of Confederate soldiers had come screaming out of the forests and had fallen on a surprised Union army. The 7th were immediately ordered forward to engage the enemy.

The weight of the opening attack fell on Grant's divisions. Fortunately for the Union, the attacking force had run into a patrol who had managed to get word back in time for some kind of defence to be quickly cobbled together. Nevertheless the Union were taken by surprise and many men were shot dead in their tents. The fighting was confused and men were accidentally killed by their own soldiers. Union men bolted and ran toward the river. Others fought in the woods. The Union fared badly and for the most part were driven back. But some areas were being violently contested. The Hornet's Nest was the name given to a sunken road that acted as a natural trench where the fighting was fiercest. Confederates were gunned down in droves as they crossed the open space between the treeline of the forest and the entrenchment. Union men were torn to bits by Confederate canon. The field that divided them caught fire and both sides could do little but listen as many of their wounded were burned alive in front of them.

Henry Smith and the 7th fought alongside the 2nd, the 12th and the 14th Iowa. The 12th and the 14th were the first to be attacked and they drove back their enemies. The Confederates regrouped and attacked the line. All four regiments felt the brunt of the assault now and were forced to repel the Confederates three more times. Henry Smith and the 7th fought solidly for six hours before they were ordered to fall back. Bullets rained on the 7th in a dangerous crossfire, killing one of their Generals as they conceded ground. The 12th and 14th were cut off and captured. Smith's battle reconvened on a nearby road where the 7th joined an impromptu force that held the line until the sun went down.

Elsewhere General Sherman travelled the length of his lines bolstering and encouraging his men. Grant had been busy reorganizing battered brigades and sending stragglers back to the fighting. The Confederate commander General Albert Sidney Johnston had been killed, bleeding to death from a minor wound that he had neglected to have properly treated.

During the night both armies were exhausted and did little fighting. Artillery bombardments continued throughout the evening. A storm raged. To Henry Smith, soaked to the skin under the heavy rain, the sound of thunder and canon fire would have been almost indistinguishable. He was surrounded by the dead and the wounded that cluttered up the twelve-mile front. Those who had been shot or bayoneted but were still alive and lying among the trees were now at the mercy of wild pigs who had come out of the woods looking for meat and did not discriminate between the living and the dead.

Twenty-five thousand reinforcements poured in from steam boats to strengthen the Union lines during the night. The following day the Union hit back at their enemies. Henry Smith

William Tecumseh Sherman.

and the 7th Iowa charged a field gun and captured it. The 7th fought until midday when Confederate resistance broke and the Confederate soldiers fled the field. The Southern retreat was echoed along the lines of battle. Although the Confederates had left, the Union were hardly in a place to claim any significant victory, being too mauled to pursue their enemies. Smith returned to camp that evening. He ate a hot meal, the first any of the 7th had eaten in two days. When night fell Smith and his compatriots slept on the ground. They had tents but they had been seconded to shelter the wounded. Over 4,000 soldiers had been killed and 2,000 more would die of their injuries. A further 16,000 had been wounded.

Sherman and Grant had made inexcusable errors that had contributed greatly to the casualty roster. But Shiloh had woken them up to the realities of the type of war they would have to wage if they were to win. It bolstered in both men a fidelity to an all-encompassing form of warfare that involved attrition and the demolition of the South's economy and infrastructure. Before long Henry Smith would be fighting under Sherman as the General put his philosophies of total war into action.

After Shiloh the Southern force, now under the command of General Beauregard, had retreated to Corinth. The 7th Iowa advanced on Corinth on 27 April. The Union armies' approach was tentative. Smith and the 7th dug trenches in preparation for a difficult and messy siege. But by June news reached them that the Confederates had abandoned Corinth. The 7th gave chase but stopped pursuing their enemies when they reached Boonville, Missouri. They returned to Corinth but remained two miles outside of the town. The 7th had respite from fighting for the rest of the summer. Whether Smith entered Corinth is not known. If he didn't, he was spared the sight of more Southern dead and wounded survivors of Shiloh, finished off by disease. During a presumably tense but passive summer of drill and guard duty, on 4 July 1862, Henry Smith was promoted to First Sergeant.

By December 1863 Smith had been fighting for two years and qualified for veteran status. He was effectively being given the opportunity to leave the army, officially having done his duty, and return to civilian life if he wanted to. Henry Smith re-enlisted on Christmas Day. In March 1864 he was promoted to Second Lieutenant. In July he was to take part in the Siege of Atlanta and its contentious aftermath under the leadership of General Sherman.

Like Grant, Sherman was a veteran of an earlier conflict having fought against the Seminole Indians. He had been a broker and lawyer. Prior to the outbreak of war he was running a military school in Louisiana. When the state went with the South, Sherman stepped down and offered his services to the North.

By 1864, after a multitude of arduous battles, the war had slowly begun to favour the North. Sherman and Grant had long ago both shaken off the disgrace of Shiloh and had earned the confidence of the President as fighting Generals. In fact Grant now commanded the entire Union Army. In this capacity he had ordered Sherman to engage and destroy the army of Tennessee under the command of General Joseph E. Johnston. Taking the city of Atlanta was the key to the North's success. Atlanta was the centre of Southern mass production. It was a gigantic repository for Southern ammunition and a crucial railway junction. It was also heavily fortified. Throughout June Sherman had pushed the Confederate forces back. The Union Army were camped within five miles of Atlanta.

General Johnston was suspected of capitulating to his enemies and was relieved of command. His replacement was John Bell Hood, a one-armed, one-legged soldier who had to be tied into the saddle of his horse during battle. Hood was an attacking General and completely the wrong sort of man to be conducting the defences in a strategically pivotal siege. From 20-28 July, Hood threw wave after wave of soldiers at the Union army when he should have been consolidated his defences, making his enemies come to him and spend the lives of their own men trying to take the city. Eighteen thousand Confederate soldiers died in three days of fighting. The 7th Iowa fought and distinguished themselves during this period of fighting.

The siege in August was defined by a sustained and pitiless artillery barrage on Atlanta. Hood felt this to be entirely unchivalrous as civilians were being killed and their homes destroyed. He even complained to Sherman whose response was to intensify the bombardment.

Sherman was putting his policy of total war into effect. He believed that to defeat an army in the field was not enough so long as there was an economy, societal infrastructure and *esprit de corps* to send new armies into the field. 'War is cruelty', he would say, and until his enemy could be rendered wholly incapable of waging war, then he considered the unthinkable acceptable if it achieved the necessary end. It was a lesson that had its roots in Shiloh.

Hood abandoned Atlanta in September. At large, he commanded a mobile army of 40,000 and was still an active threat as he engaged in a hit-and-run war against Sherman. The Union General wanted to pursue his philosophy of total war to its logical conclusion. Less concerned with checking Hood, he proposed to march through Georgia laying waste to everything of value to the Southern economy. President Lincoln balked at the idea. Even Grant was reluctant to let Sherman have his way, but was ultimately convinced and in turn persuaded the president. Sherman split his force. He left soldiers enough to tackle Hood and kept 62,000 men for himself. Sherman set fire to Atlanta and on 15 November began his march through Georgia.

Sherman's army averaged ten miles a day, destroying the land at a leisurely pace. What food they did not raze they ate themselves. Resistance was marginal and insignificant. The campaign was virtually uncontested. The attitude among the soldiers seemed blithe as they effectively starved the state of Georgia into submission.

It is unlikely that Henry Smith was remotely conflicted about any of this as he marched with Sherman. Virtually all of the General's men were in accord with his doctrine of total war. All of Sherman's soldiers were hardened campaigners by this stage. Smith and the 7th Iowa were clearly not the same novices who had fought at Belmont. They had experienced pitched battles and numerous skirmishes. Smith had witnessed unimaginable suffering. He had nearly been killed himself and had invariably killed others. One of the many effects of years of this sort of fighting would have been an inevitable degree of calcification in regard to the afflictions of his enemies.

The 7th Iowa had marched with Sherman until 10 December. They were not present with him when he reached the sea on 13th of the same month. The Union had caused $100 million worth of damage to Georgia. The war was nearing its conclusion and its closing melees would offer Henry Smith his greatest opportunity for personal glorification.

Four months later Henry Smith and 7th Iowa were in North Carolina. On 15 March at seven o'clock in the morning the 7th left camp. Their destination was the Black River. Their objective was to drive a group of Confederates away from a nearby bridge. The 7th reached the river at two in the afternoon and set up camp. Two hours later they received orders to cross the river. They waited for the sun to go down and left camp. Henry Smith and the 7th stopped their advance three quarters of a mile from the bridge. They set about building a makeshift pontoon that would take them across the Black River. The river was powerful and worked against the Union men's efforts. The Confederates, fully aware of the presence of the enemy soldiers, opened fire. Near to Henry Smith a man was pulled away by the current and swept down river. Smith removed his sword and took off his coat. He dived into the river and swam after the drowning man. He caught hold of him and began to swim back to a place of safety all the while under fire from Confederate troops.

Pretty soon most of the 7th were drenched. On the far side of the river much of the surrounding swamp land had flooded and was shoulder deep in places. A sodden regiment moved through the trees trying to connect with the road that would take them to the Confederate defences and battle. When they arrived the enemy position had been abandoned. Henry Smith and the 7th slept in their wet clothes. They had no blankets or food. Their commanding officer praised the way his men endured discomfort and did not complain.

Throughout the spring and summer months of that final year of warfare the Confederate forces had been surrendering in increments. The war was drawing to a close. On 6 July 1865 Henry Smith was made a captain. Six days later he was mustered out of the army. His career as a soldier was at an end.

During the Civil War a new medal had been created for acts of courage performed by members of the Union armed forces. Initially the medal was for navy personnel only but the law was changed to allow the members of army to become eligible. Henry Smith's conduct at the Black River made him the only native of Nottingham ever to win the Congressional Medal of Honour. Emblematic of extreme courage, the Medal has gone on to become the most coveted military honour in the American armed forces.

After the war Smith went back to farming. He did not actually receive his medal until 1894. By the time he was eventually allowed to hold it in his hands he was a married man; had become a county treasurer and had helped establish the First National Bank in Mason City where he would reside until his death. His last years were dogged by illness. In 1910, on 12 November, he died. His body was interred in Elmwood St Joseph's Cemetery in Iowa. The bullet from the wound he had received in Belmont fort-nine years previously was still lodged in his shoulder.

NINE

◇◇

Five Soldiers

Nottingham and Victoria's Wars

Perhaps the most celebrated battle of the entire Victorian era was the defence of Rorke's Drift in 1879, during which a tiny handful of British soldiers fought off an army of 4,000 or so Zulu warriors. The battle became justifiably famous for the record number of Victoria Crosses that were awarded to the defenders. Eleven VCs for a single action remains a tally as yet unsurpassed in British military history. The array of deeds that earned the VC at Rorke's Drift was an incredible miscellany of rescues, assaults, feats of endurance and outstanding leadership. Three Nottinghamshire men fought in the battle. Not one of them won the Victoria Cross, but as part of the anonymous majority of soldiers, whose collective discipline determined the defenders survival, their contribution to the battle was vital. All three men came from, or had at some point settled in, the village of Ruddington on the outskirts of Nottingham. Their names were Caleb Wood, Robert Tongue and James Marshall.

The irony of Rorke's Drift is that it was a battle that should never have happened, was of no strategic advantage to the enemy and was fought in a war that had not been sanctioned by the British Government. The defenders of Rorke's Drift were soldiers that had been left behind for the initial stages of the war, under the command of officers who were considered ordinary and past their prime. In the days leading up to the battle Wood, Tongue and Marshall would have seen something close to 5,000 soldiers pass through the Drift in preparation for the invasion of Zululand.

The war had effectively been started by one man, the British High Commissioner for South Africa, Sir Bartle Frere. Frere was uneasy to the point of paranoia about the presence of the Zulu people so close to British territories. The Zulu army comprised 40,000 highly skilled warriors. Zulu culture was rooted in the military, its history being one of warfare, conquest and expansion; a Zulu male was not allowed to marry until he had proved himself in combat. With such warlike neighbours Sir Bartle Frere felt that conflict with the Zulus was inevitable. His policy was one of pre-emption and he was keen to invade the Zululand before the Zulus took it upon themselves to attack British interests.

The Zulus were easily the most disciplined, well led and formidable native fighting force in the southern regions of the African continent. Under their great leader, Shaka, they had invaded and dominated the territory before the arrival in force of the first Europeans. In recent times there had been violence and bloodshed between the Zulus and the Dutch, who alongside

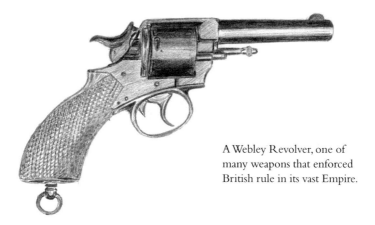

A Webley Revolver, one of many weapons that enforced British rule in its vast Empire.

the British, were the other significant white presence in the region. Yet the reigning Zulu King, Cetshwayo, had little desire to start a war with Britain. He had some notion of the scale and power of the British Empire and had the foresight to see that the technological advantages in terms of firearms at Britain's disposal would make war a suicidal course of action for his people. For his part, Frere had been ordered by London to tread lightly and diplomatically as far as the Zulus were concerned. The British had trouble in Afghanistan and the Balkans and did not need another expensive war if it was at all avoidable.

The speed of communication between London and Cape Town was sluggish. Frere took advantage of this and set about trying to provoke the Zulu King to war. And if the war was won quickly and decisively, before Frere's plans could be vetoed by the British government, then he would be a hero, having prompted and averted a crisis, forcing his detractors to hold their tongues. Frere punished the Zulus for making minor infringements of any of the treaties that stood with the Europeans with a disproportionate and provocative vigour. He made heavy demands for restitution from the Zulu King, ultimately insisting that Cetshwayo disband his army. The King had been as compliant as he could be on everything up to this point but the last demand he refused. Insisting that a Zulu King disband his army was tantamount to asking the Zulus to stop being Zulus. Frere had his pretext to go to war.

Rorke's Drift was a mission station consisting of two thatched stone buildings, constituting a church and living quarters for missionaries. The church was used by the army for storage while the living quarters doubled as a hospital. Thirty-five sick languished in the hospital.

On 22 January 1879 the last column left Rorke's Drift. The remaining force, comprising B Company of the 24th Regiment of Foot (including the sick and not counting native levies), numbered 139 Europeans soldiers. Their function at Rorke's Drift was to wait to be relieved by soldiers saddled with the mundane task of constructing a stone fort that would guard the Drift. They would then be free to join the main force. Caleb Wood, Robert Tongue and James Marshall would most likely have been relaxing as their commanding officer, Lieutenant John Rouse Merriot Chard, had effectively given his soldiers the morning off.

Around midday the three Ruddinton men may have been among those who heard the distant sound of gunfire. It wouldn't have alarmed them particularly. The war had begun as expected and the British were obviously prosecuting their technological superiority against a numerically superior but technologically primitive foe.

By mid-afternoon two riders approached Rorke's Drift. They quickly dismounted and were very soon in frantic conference with the Drift's commanding officers, Lieutenant Chard and Lieutenant Gonville Bromhead. Shortly afterward the men were assembled. The Ruddington soldiers heard the shocking news that their regiment had been all but massacred on the plains of Isandlwana. A force of 14,000 Zulus had defeated 1,700 British and loyal native soldiers, killing 1,300 of them. A section of the Zulu army (or 'impi' as it was know) had broken away and was headed toward Rorke's Drift with the intention of destroying the mission station and its inhabitants. Orders were quickly issued to make the mission as defensible as possible. Flight was pointless as the Zulus were notoriously fast overland and didn't take prisoners. A frenetic period of activity followed. The main bulk of the work was hefting 200lb sacks and 112lb boxes to make walls and barricades. Wagons were overturned and loopholes were smashed into the hospital walls.

The force at Rorke's Drift was a fraction of the size of the one slaughtered at Isandlwana. It must have crossed the defenders minds at some point that what they were doing was futile. Yet the defenders' morale received a tremendous boost by the unexpected arrival of 350 armed horsemen. They were survivors of Isandlwana, Basutu soldiers who had served under the Brevet Colonel Anthony Durnford, who been killed during the battle. The defender's strength had swelled significantly and for a moment their prospects of survival would have looked almost optimistic.

A lookout announced that the Zulus had been spotted. Before long Wood, Tongue and Marshall would have got a sense of the size of the force that was coming against them. In excess of 4,000 warriors were running toward the mission station. The Zulus were fresh to battle having been amongst those who had not had the chance to fight at Isandwlana. In fact their failure to shed blood was their principle reason for assaulting the garrison at Rorke's Drift. Initiated and led by the Zulu Prince Dabulamanzi kaMpande, it was a virtually independent assault and one that had not been ordered by the Zulu King.

Ammunition was passed around. The Ruddington men stuffed their pouches and pockets with cartridges. The order was given and they fixed their bayonets.

The newly arrived reinforcement left almost as soon as they had arrived. The horsemen lost their nerve and rode away. A large band of native levies joined them. Wood, Tongue and Marshall heard shots. Some of their own men had opened fire on the fleeing Basutus. They would have quickly become aware that a European Sergeant accompanying the Basutus had been hit in the back and was dead, and that their own officers had conspicuously turned a blind eye to the killing.

At around four o'clock in the afternoon the Zulus were visible. The three Ruddington men each placed a bullet into their single shot Martini Henry rifles and waited for the order to fire. The Zulus charged. Wood, Tongue and Marshall took aim and pulled their triggers. They worked the levers of their rifles, ejecting the used cartridges, inserting a fresh cartridge and pulling the trigger again, absorbed in the wave of volley fire which killed numerous Zulus but which didn't seem to halt their momentum as they crashed into the Drift's defences.

The British fighting technique was to crouch to fire and then stand and stab with their bayonets. The Zulus sought to grab the defenders barrels and stab back at them with their assegai spears or else crack their heads open with their knobkerrie clubs. Zulus were notoriously bad marksmen but they had guns and their snipers poured inaccurate but hazardous fire into

A British soldier engages a Zulu warrior at the battle of Rorke's Drift.

Rorke's Drift. Although the shots were poorly aimed, the volume of fire took its toll and here and there defenders were clipped and wounded or killed when a stray round struck them. Above the frenetic sounds of hand-to-hand combat Wood, Tongue and Marshall heard their chaplain shouting verses from the Bible over the din of battle, contributing to the increasingly apocalyptic soundscape.

The fighting continued for an hour before the Zulus disengaged. In the respite between assaults the Ruddington men may have been conscious of the strange paradox in the Zulus' fighting style. The Zulus had rushed face first into volley fire but seemed almost coy when engaging the bayonet. Their hesitancy had – as VC winner Frederick Hitch would later observe – probably saved Rorke's Drift from being overwhelmed and the defenders massacred.

The assaults continued. Defensive walls collapsed and the perimeter began to contract. The Zulus focused a huge amount of their attention on storming and torching the hospital. By six o'clock in the evening the attackers began to gain ground in and around the hospital. Within the infirmary walls some of the most intense and savage fighting of the battle was taking place. Wood, Tongue and Marshall didn't see it for themselves but experienced its after-effects as the heat of the now blazing hospital could be palpably felt. The surviving inhabitants and defenders of the hospital assault fled for the relative safety of the barricades, freeing more Zulus to attack what was left of the defences.

Three of Rorke's Drift veterans are buried in the same graveyard in Ruddington.

Come night time the Ruddington men and their compatriots occupied the last defensible position. If it fell they would all be killed. They were exhausted. Their faces were most likely stained black by powder burns. They would have been, at the very least, bruised from hours of repetitive hand-to-hand combat and possibly cut and bleeding from the stabs and slashes of their enemies. Their hands and their cheeks were singed and blistered due to the overheated rifles they had been forced to fire time and time again. Worst of all, they were incredibly thirsty. The only real source of refreshment was the water cart which was on the other side of the perimeter, and unless somebody went into the black and faced the Zulus in the open there would be virtually nothing to drink. At midnight Chard took a detachment of men to get the water cart. The risky and potentially fatal expedition was a success and afforded Wood, Tongue and Marshall perhaps the sweetest drink of water they would ever taste.

The battle carried on in its former intensity for a couple more hours and then the fight seemed to go out of the enemy and the pace of the battle slackened. Everyone would have had to continue to be careful as snipers were still taking pot shots and assegais were being thrown over the parapets. The Ruddington men craved sleep. Their officers ordered the defenders to keep active and put them to work breaking down the walls of the gutted hospital and removing combustible thatch from the roofs. But the battle was over. The last few hours of night were silent. As the sun came up Wood, Tongue and Marshall were confronted with the scale of what they had been part of. Fifteen of their own men were dead. Two more were dying in the infirmary. The ground was covered in many thousands of spent cartridges. Rorke's Drift was surrounded by heaps of dead and dying Zulu warriors. The three soldiers may have been aware of the presence of their own countrymen moving among the Zulu dead in search of survivors and heard the shots that followed as they killed the wounded.

The three Nottingham veterans were all buried in the same Ruddington cemetery. The reward for their service was obscurity. Caleb Wood and Robert Tongue's graves had no headstone and Marshall's bore no reference to his participation in the battle.

Between 2004 and 2008, after a passionate campaign from academics and military history enthusiasts, all three soldiers were granted new or restored headstones. The words, 'Rorke's Drift Defender' were cut into each of them.

If the Victoria Cross had eluded the three Ruddington men, that wasn't to be the case for Ruddington-born Francis Wheatley. Whealtley was the son of a Framework knitter. He joined the First Battalion Rifle Brigade on 5 November 1839 and in 1854 was part of the combined British, French and Turkish coalition that came together to fight Russian forces in the Crimea.

As far as Britain was concerned, the war with Russia was a territorial dispute over who had naval dominance in the Mediterranean. The French and the Turks had different reasons for going to war but the three countries were united in their desire to drive Russia out of the Crimea. On many levels the war was a hesitantly commanded and badly administered affair. Timidity in both the pursuit of a defeated Russian force at the battle of Alma and an assault on the fortress of Sebastopol robbed the invading coalition of a potentially quick victory. It forced the war to become a conflict defined by protracted artillery duels, barrages of shot and shell, and tunnel and trench warfare. British soldiers entered the conflict without adequate clothing for the Russian climate and countryside and would become victims of an appalling winter that would freeze, mutilate and kill many of them. It was in this context of frozen siege warfare and horrific privation that Francis Wheatley won his Victoria Cross on 10 November 1854 at Sebastopol.

An artillery shell had landed in Francis Wheatley's trench. He took his rifle and smashed away at the fuse of the shell trying to deactivate it. It didn't work. The shell would detonate soon and if something wasn't done it was unlikely that Wheatley or his fellow soldiers would get out of the way in time to avoid being killed or maimed by the imminent explosion. Wheatley picked the shell up and heaved it out of the trench. The shell exploded. Wheatley and his companions' lives were saved.

The Victoria Cross was invented in 1856 to reward those who had distinguished themselves in outstanding feats of combat, sacrifice or exemplary execution of military duty in the face of the enemy. It was a meritocratic decoration open to any rank provided they had survived (posthumous VCs were permitted later). The Victoria Cross was made from metal taken from canons captured at Sebastopol. The first batch of medals were presented in person by Queen Victoria in Hyde Park on 26 June 1857. Francis Wheatley was one of an initial sixty-two recipients to receive the decoration from the Queen who sat on her horse and leaned down to pin the medal on the Ruddington soldier's chest.

The Crimea was seen as one of the first modern conflicts of the nineteenth century, prefiguring the First World War in its reliance on heavy technology, trench combat and sustained artillery bombardments. The fighting was as brutal as any war but punctuated by the odd moment of chivalry. Fellow VC winner Captain Henry Clifford, after beheading a Russian soldier and chopping another's arm off at the battle of Inkerman found himself on excellent speaking terms the following day with his surviving victim. But immediately after the Crimea

Soldiers in Nottingham's Market Place make ready to leave for the Crimea. (Courtesy of G.H.F. Atkins and www.picturethepast.org.uk)

Captured Russian guns decorate the Sebastopol monument in the Arboretum, paying tribute to the achievements of Nottingham soldiers in the Crimean War.

came a conflict that was diametrically opposite in nature, typified by atrocity on both sides, deep-rooted racial hatred and hand-to-hand fighting about as primitive and medieval as the nineteenth century would allow. And toward the tail end of the struggle another Nottingham man would win another Victoria Cross.

In India the introduction of a new paper cartridge among the native soldiers (or sepoys) who fought for the British became the pretext for a rebellion that almost cost the Empire one its most vital acquisitions. About 80 per cent of the Crown's armed forces in India were indigenous, drawn from Sikh, Moslem and Hindu soldier castes. The cartridge was designed for use in the brand new Enfield rifles the British intended to equip all of their soldiers in India with. In order to pour the gunpowder contained in the cartridge into the barrel of the rifle, a soldier would be required to bite off the end of the cartridge. Rumours had begun to circulate that the cartridges had been greased with the fat of pigs or cows, a deeply blasphemous notion to the majority of sepoys, pig fat being sacrilegious to Moslems and cow fat to Hindus.

The fear was unfounded. The British never used pig or cow fat, or else remedied their mistake before the tainted cartridges were ever issued to sepoys. But there was a willingness among many to believe the rumour which tapped into a deep well of longstanding resentment that had remained barely latent among the native armed forces and large swathes of the civilian population.

Bitterness against inroads Christian missionaries had made in their attempts to bring the gospel to India was rife. The double standards that dictated how a European and how an Indian soldier could be promoted rankled, as did various changes in army administration that took little or no account of religious sensitivities. In 1834 lower caste Sikhs and Moslems were allowed to join the Bengal Army. This offended the high-caste sepoys who traditionally constituted the backbone of the Indian armed forces. Further insult was added in 1856 when the General Service Enlistment Order dictated that sepoys would have to serve abroad and in doing so would be subject to contamination from proximity to lower caste individuals. But the most explosive piece of legislation was the Doctrine of Lapse, which decreed that if the ruler of a province died without leaving an heir then the British were entitled to annex their lands. Worse was to come. The annexation of the northern Kingdom of Oudh was particularly contentious and worrying to sepoy and civilian alike. Wajid Ali was the ruler of Oudh and perceived to be an immoral and sexually profligate man by his Victorian contemporaries, so Oudh was annexed on the grounds of immorality.

The British administration naively misunderstood the volatile levels of ill feeling that the annexation provoked. They also failed to take into consideration the question of odds. Eight out of ten soldiers in the Indian Army were sepoys and 75,000 sepoys came from Oudh. So when rumours of a tainted cartridge began to circulate there was a frightening groundswell of armed and resentful sepoys more than ready to believe ill of their masters and act on their worst suspicions.

In February 1857 groups of sepoys started refusing to use the greased cartridges. In March a sepoy named Mungal Pandy opened fire on his adjutant and sergeant major. He was hanged. In May, at Meerut, eighty-five sepoys of the Bengal Light Cavalry were arrested for refusing to use the new cartridges. Their punishment was severe: each of them was given ten years hard labour. On 9 May they were displayed in irons on the garrison parade ground. The next day the sepoys at Meerut rebelled. They killed fifty Europeans including many of their own officers and their wives and children. The mutineers marched on to Delhi, murdering Europeans as they came across them.

The rebellion at Meerut was replicated on a much larger scale at Dehli. The city fell to the mutineers. More Europeans were killed and all surviving whites fled for their lives. Lucknow (Oudh's capital) and Cawnpore were the other major cities to be wrested from the control of the British. Each territorial gain was accompanied by more indiscriminate killing. In Lucknow and Cawnpore surviving pockets of British resistance managed to hold off their attackers in fortified residences; they were besieged, cut off from outside help and subject to relentless artillery bombardments, assaults, disease and the gradual diminishing of supplies.

The surviving force at Lucknow held out and waited to be relieved believing that any capitulation to the mutineers would result in their deaths. Cawnpore had suffered horribly at the hands of their attackers and agreed to terms for an honourable withdrawal. They were permitted to leave with their weapons and a promise of safe passage to boats waiting for them on the banks of the River Ganges.

Whether they were deliberately betrayed, or heightened tensions on both sides sparked an avoidable confrontation is still a matter for debate. At any rate a gun went off. The British believed they were under attack and opened fire. The British were shot dead and cut down.

If the gun battle was an accident, what happened next was undoubtedly premeditated. The female survivors of Cawnpore and their children were spared and imprisoned at Bibigarh.

But later in the conflict, as the tide began to turn against the mutineers and the British relief expeditions made headway against them, the order was given to kill the Cawnpore survivors. The women and children were cut and hacked to death and their bodies thrown down a well.

It was in this context of relief expeditions and brutal retaliation that Samuel Morley fought against the mutinous sepoys. Once the back of the mutiny had been broken, it was in the act of mopping up the final pockets of resistance that the Nottingham soldier won his Victoria Cross.

Samuel Morley was born in 1829 in East Retford, Nottinghamshire. He originally served with the 8th Hussars and was present in the Crimea before being posted to India. He had been transferred to the 2nd Battalion of the Military Train and was part of the second attempt to relieve Lucknow under the leadership of the gifted soldier and hero of the Crimea, Sir Colin Campbell.

The first attempt to rescue the besieged garrison had been partially successfully. Under Major General Sir Henry James Outrum the relief force had lost so many men fighting their way to the residency that they lacked the strength of numbers to evacuate the defenders. They chose to stay and reinforced the residency instead. They captured and occupied the fortress of the Alambagh nearby, and waited with their fellow besieged to be relieved themselves.

Samuel Morley arrived at Lucknow in November 1857 with a relief force bolstered by soldiers who had been rerouted from China to deal with the Indian crisis. The Alambagh was relived. The women and children at the residency were evacuated straight away. The besieged troops followed shortly afterward.

The city of Lucknow was still occupied and had yet to be taken. With the exception of Lucknow, all the major strongholds under rebel control had been retaken. The cost in terms of lives lost to both sides had been devastating. The character of the fighting had been bitter street combat. Since news of the massacres at Cawnpore had become general knowledge, any pretence at civility was abandoned. Few prisoners were taken by either side. The British murdered many Indians, hanging them without trial and little thought or care as to whether they had anything to do with the mutiny or not. At Cawnpore, Indian prisoners were forced to clean up the blood of the murdered women and children before being executed (in some instances being made to lick the blood up), an act, according to their religion, that would damn them to hell.

Consequently the fighting at Lucknow to relieve the residency was embittered. Not much mercy was shown. 'Remember Cawnpore' was the oft heard battle cry as Campbell's forces shot, stabbed and cut their way to their besieged countrymen and women.

The main assault on Lucknow was delayed. Campbell was needed back at Cawnpore where there was a fresh eruption of rebel activity to be dealt with. Samuel Morley was among the 4,000 soldiers who stayed behind at the Alambagh under the command of Outrum. In the interim, between the relief of the residency and the final assault on Lucknow, the rebels' numbers increased from 30,000 to 100,000 defenders, a mixture of mutinous professionals and armed civilians.

The final attack on Lucknow came in March 1858. The fighting lasted from the 2nd to the 21st. The city eventually fell to the British (whose ranks were augmented by many loyal native soldiers) after a typically savage campaign. Samuel Morley took part in the battle.

In spite of the ruthlessness displayed by the British, Sir Colin Campbell was content to chase the defenders out of the city rather than rout them completely. The war was effectively won and the mutiny had been contained to the north of the country. But Sir Colin Campbell's decision not to press his victory at Lucknow ensured that his soldiers would be tackling itinerate bands of dangerous rebels throughout the rest of the year.

In the Spring the army was reorganised into the Azamgarh, Lucknow and Rohilcund All Arms Field Forces. Samuel Morley was assigned to Azamgarh.

On 15 April 1858 Private Morley and an Irish Sergeant named Michael Murphy were part of a squadron comprising members of the Military Train, the Horse Artillery and the 3rd Sikh Cavalry. They were in pursuit of a band of mutineers. In the melèe that followed, the rebels unhorsed a Lieutenant Hamilton. A mutineer shot Morley's horse and killed it beneath him. As the lieutenant lay on the floor a group of sepoys surrounded him and began to slash and hack at his body.

The favoured weapon in hand-to-hand combat among the sepoys was the tulwar: a slight, curved and extraordinarily sharp blade. A skilful man wielding a tulwar was capable of inflicting incredible injuries on his opponent. Billy Russell, the famous war correspondent for *The Times* newspaper had seen after-effects of sword fights in the Crimea and the Indian Mutiny and was horrified at the damage a tulwar could do to the human body. The heavier and duller European swords were incapable of inflicting the same type of damage and any British soldier engaging a sepoy with a European sword was often at a serious disadvantage. The British learned to adapt and many endeavoured to master the tulwar and carried it into battle themselves.

Whether Private Morley and Sergeant Murphy were armed with tulwars is not certain. The fighting was hand-to-hand and the sepoys that died were killed at close quarters and invariably cut down. Both men fought over the injured body of the lieutenant until help arrived. Between them they killed five or six rebels. Murphy bore the brunt of the injuries, sustaining five separate wounds which required serious medical attention when the fight was over.

Elderly Nottingham veterans of the Crimean War and the Indian Mutiny. (Courtesy of Nottingham City Council and www.picturethepast.org.uk

Samuel Morley and Michael Murphy fight to save a wounded lieutenant during the latter stages of the Indian Mutiny. Both men won the Victoria Cross for their part in the action.

The tombstone of Samuel Morley.

In all probability Murphy killed more men than his Nottingham compatriot – a single dead sepoy being directly attributed to Morley – but both men shared the incredible risk and would most likely have been killed had the other not been there to support and protect his fellow soldier. However, neither was able to save Hamilton who died a day later as a result of his injuries.

Michael Murphy was recommended for the Victoria Cross but Morley was overlooked. A year later, when it was announced that Murphy would receive the VC, Morley was incensed. During a parade he complained to General Lord Alfred Pagent. His claim was investigated and on 7 August 1860 the army agreed that he had done enough to warrant the medal. He received his decoration in person from Queen Victoria at Windsor.

TEN

◇◇

'Every minute of his crowded life'

Albert Ball and the War in the Air

The mechanised slaughter in the muddy trenches of the First World War was military conflict stripped of even the slightest veneer of romanticism. The machinery of martial propaganda desperately needed heroes to uplift a shocked nation's dented morale. If they couldn't be found on the ground then the sky would have to do.

Fighter pilots' contribution to the overall strategic ebb and flow of the war was never that significant. But fighter pilots were flamboyant, individualistic and easily lent themselves to the sort mythologising that mitigated against the horrors of trench combat. Nottingham's Albert Ball was one of the first great English air aces of the First World War.

The aeroplane's initial usage in the early stages of the conflict was hardly glamorous, its primary function being the gathering of intelligence and the monitoring of artillery bombardments. But as German and Allied Forces began to embrace the use of aircraft in this manner, each side sought to develop their own methods of destroying the other's planes. The first examples of aerial combat were crude and improvised. Pilots shot at each other with hand guns, flying at close quarters. This didn't last long. Planes were quickly adapted to fire machine guns and pilots started being trained in a more rarefied form of aerial warfare. It was this type of fighting and the glory it promised that would fire the imagination of an eighteen-year-old Albert Ball who volunteered to fight for his country on 21 September 1914.

Albert Ball was the son of a Lenton plumber who had become an alderman and then mayor of Nottingham, his uncle would also become mayor one year later. Albert's parents were sufficiently well off to pay to send their boy to Trent College, a patriotic Anglican school. Albert Ball was not particularly academic, being especially bad at spelling, but he did show a great aptitude for mechanics, a talent which the school fostered. Trent College also drummed into its students the importance of physical fitness and martial duty. Both interests converged in Albert Ball's choice of hobbies. He loved pistols, was a keen collector, and by all accounts a very good marksman. Albert Ball could also seemingly mend the most decrepit piece of old machinery and restore it to something close to its former glory. When he left school a career in an electrical company seemed the best way to utilise his talents until war broke out and Albert Ball enlisted in the Army.

For Albert Ball, enlisting in the armed forces was a race against time. He desperately wanted to get to France fast enough to experience the excitement and glamour of action before the

Albert Ball.

war ended. When Albert joined up the war was scarcely two months old and like many people he thought it would be over far too quickly for him to leave any kind of personal imprint. Albert Ball joined the Sherwood Forresters. He was promoted quickly, making sergeant and then second lieutenant by October. He was transferred to Ealing as part of the North Midlands Division Cyclists. It was in Ealing that he saw military aircraft and decided that he wanted to join the Royal Flying Corps.

As a preparatory measure Albert Ball took private flying lessons. He trained at the Ruffy Beauman School. He took lessons in his own time and at his own expense (spending a total of £75) fitting private tuition around his demanding military routine. The work that he had put in did not immediately pay dividends when he eventually embarked on his official military flight training. He loved flying but wasn't, at least to start with, a natural pilot, crashing his aircraft on only his third flight. He also saw the ugly inverse of the glory that he believed waited for him in France when he observed the bloody aftermath of a crash. A 2in piece of wood had pierced the head of a downed trainee pilot who would die of the injuries sustained in the accident.

On 15 October 1915 Albert Ball qualified as a pilot. He was transferred to the Royal Flying Corps and underwent further training in Norwich. On 22 January 1916 he received his wings. His first assignment was as an instructor for No. 22 squadron. He was sent to France just as the Somme Offensive had begun to take effect and was assigned to No. 13 Squadron. To begin with Albert Ball flew the slow and workmanlike BE2c on reconnaissance missions, as well as the odd bombing raid. He was still not thought of as a particularly skilful pilot. His superiors even considered sending him back to England for further training. Ironically what saved him from the humiliation of a return trip home was engine failure. Albert Ball was forced to land his BE2c when its engine packed in. The downed pilot put his mechanical acumen to work and repaired the plane sufficiently to splutter slowly back to base. By the time he reached safety it had become evident that in order to get back to base the young pilot had spent a night out in the cold with his plane and had flown through a snow storm. This mixture of improvisation and determination impressed his superiors sufficiently for Albert Ball to be kept on.

In late March, Albert Ball experienced aerial combat for the first time. He was on a spotting mission in a two-seater aircraft. Ball had extraordinarily good eyesight and saw enemy planes a considerable distance away. His observer controlled the plane's machine gun and together they attacked the two German aircraft. It was a brave but inconclusive contest. Yet it was significant in that the Nottingham pilot realised what he had probably suspected all along: he hated reconnaissance and loved to fly and fight alone. Around the same time Ball had his first flight in a Bristol Scout, a single-seater aircraft that was fashioned after civilian racing planes. It was lightly armoured but comparatively fast, travelling at 93mph, and very much to Albert Ball's liking.

Ball's determination to gain combat experience saw him volunteer to fly on lengthy reconnaissance missions in his own time, a pretext for looking for a fight with the enemy. He made a nuisance of himself pestering Command to fly the Bristol. They agreed. But Albert Ball only got to fly his beloved Bristol a few times before another pilot crashed it. The Bristol's replacement nearly killed him when he accidentally shot off his own propeller with an uncalibrated machine gun.

On 7 May Albert Ball was transferred to No. 11 Squadron, a fighting unit using perhaps the best aircraft Britain ever employed during the First World War. The Niueport 17 could fly for two hours. Its speed was 102mph. It could climb 2,000ft in seven seconds. It was extremely manoeuvrable and provided the pilot with excellent visibility. It also came fitted with the powerful Lewis Gun placed above the pilot on the top wing of the biplane. The Lewis Gun was an American weapon rejected in its country of origin but embraced in Europe. Its rate of fire was formidable, expending up to 500 in a minute. Its magazine sat on the top of the weapon and held ninety-seven rounds.

Albert Ball would come to idolise the Nieuport 17 but it was in a Bristol Scout that he scored his first victory. On 15 May he spotted a German Albatross aircraft. Ball was 7,000ft above his target. He took his plane into a dive and fired one hundred and twenty rounds at the Albatross. The enemy plane crashed but Albert Ball could not claim the victory for himself. A witness had to verify the kill for it to be officially credited to him. It must have galled him slightly but it was a moot point. Over the next few months he would have plenty of opportunities and numerous witnesses that would add kill after kill to his tally. His inauspicious and clumsy beginnings as a pilot were about to be supplanted by an emerging reputation as an air ace in the making.

Albert Ball clocked up his first confirmed kill in a Bristol Scout. On 22 May he tried to shoot down an Albatross but disengaged when he found himself flying too close to the ground within range of enemy guns. Later in the day he engaged another Albatross and shot it down. This time there were witnesses to verify what he had done. He tried for a third Albatross the same day but disengaged when he realised how little fuel he had left. His Bristol Scout was a mess when he landed, punched full of holes by enemy gunfire from the ground and from the sky.

At the beginning of June Albert Ball fought off a Fokker and an Albatross simultaneously. He was sent on leave for a short while. On his return he attacked and destroyed an observation kite balloon with a phosphorous grenade and was given the Military Cross. It was a frenetic and intense period of combat. It was what Albert Ball wanted and it had won him laurels, but it exacted a price. At his own request Albert Ball was posted to the less combat-intensive No. 8 Squadron. He had asked his superiors for a rest and they had agreed to the transfer. The moment Ball made the decision he seemed immediately to regret it. Rather than recuperate, he began volunteering for every mission available. And whilst with No. 8 Squadron, supposedly at rest, he launched an attack on a heavily defended observation balloon so ferocious that the occupant had to bail out. Albert Ball was sent back to No. 11 Squadron.

On 14 August, on Albert's birthday, he was allowed his own Nieuport A126, which he tended with the loving consideration of an obsessive mechanic. His Lewis gun was mounted

Ground fire peppered Albert Ball's Bristol Scout on the day he scored his first confirmed kill.

Albert Ball destroys a German observation kite balloon, winning the Military Cross in the process.

on a slide, a modification that suited his combat preferences. This meant that he could reload in the air quickly and more easily and that the weapon could be pulled down and fired vertically into a plane's undercarriage. This was becoming a signature dogfighting technique of Albert Ball. He was fond of diving under his enemies and shooting up at them, or else flying straight at them as if to collide and then shooting into the vulnerable part of the enemy aircraft when it inevitably pulled away before he did. He would deliberately allow himself to be tailed by a pursuing aircraft, would wait until the enemy was about to shoot, before disappearing and reappearing behind his opponent and opening fire. His style was unorthodox to say the least. It relied on incredible reflexes and excellent eyesight and marksmanship. It was effective but seen by some as more reliant on luck and the ability to terrorise the enemy into making fatal errors rather than any real tactical awareness. It was a fighting philosophy that many felt would inevitably result in the death of its practitioner.

On 22 August Albert Ball shot down the German Ace Willy Cymera, killing his observer and causing his plane to fall 6,000 feet. The German war hero survived but was forced to crash his aircraft into the roof of a house.

Alongside his now obvious prowess as a fighter pilot Albert Ball would also garner a reputation for eccentricity. He ate cake in the air. He flew without goggles. He lived in a tent rather than a billet. He tended a vegetable garden. He played the violin and seemed to prefer music to company. He was a loner but not a complete hermit and despite a reluctance to socialise, he was liked among his peers. But sometimes his behaviour would tip the balance from the eccentric into the bizarre, once walking around a lit flare playing his violin. His actions were often

Air Ace Albert Ball, sitting in the cockpit beneath his specially customised Lewis gun, mounted on a slide so that he could shoot up into the undercarriage of enemy fighter planes. (Courtesy of Nottingham City Council and www.picturethepast.org.uk)

symptomatic of the conduct of a man less at ease with the adrenalized world he had courted than he would care to admit.

By August Albert Ball had been awarded the Distinguished Service Order. At this stage he had been given virtual autonomy to fly and fight on his own. During September Albert Ball was hunting for observation balloons in his beloved Nieuport. The Nieuport had been fitted with rockets. Ball couldn't find a balloon but came upon a scout plane. He fired the rockets at the scout. The rockets missed. Ball turned his Lewis gun on the scout and shot it down. In the pandemonium which followed, Ball's Nieuport was badly perforated by enemy fire. He returned to base in a tattered plane damaged enough to be put out of commission for three months.

He was sent home for two weeks. King George V personally presented him with his DSO. When the fortnight had elapsed Albert Ball was back in France where he was given command of his own squadron. His tally of victories increased and a bar was added to his DSO. His time back in France was brief. It was deemed necessary to send him back to England once again to rest and to utilise his combat experience as an instructor.

Albert Ball came home a hero. He was considered, at that point, the most successful English fighter pilot of the war and its first authentic ace. He was a courted man. In Nottingham he was given the key to the city. Prime Minister David Lloyd George ate with him and he was offered £1,000 to sit on a company's board on condition that he left the Royal Flying Corps. But Albert Ball was keen to get back to France. He was once again at the behest of the same duality in his nature that had previously caused him to ask for a transfer to No. 8 Squadron on the grounds of fatigue, only to immediately regret the decision and work tirelessly to get back to a fighting squadron. There was a further complication: Albert Ball had fallen in love. The object of his affection was young lady named Flora Young and Ball's letters to her would reveal a rift in his personality regarding his private misgivings about the war. Albert Ball was a devout Christian. He prayed a great deal and credited his many escapes from death to God. He loved to fly and clearly seemed addicted to the excitement afforded by combat. Yet he never hated his enemies and felt immense personal guilt whenever he killed. The moral paradox of his beloved profession was a great torment to him.

In February 1917, on his return to France, Albert Ball was transferred to the newly minted No. 56 Squadron. The purpose of the unit was to debut the SE5 Scout. Ball was made a flight commander and despite the SE5 being the signature plane of the Squadron, was once again given his own Nieuport. Ball would alternate between the two planes throughout his next period of combat.

Albert Ball had determined that his current posting would be his last. His tour was supposed to be a month and during that month he had a personal goal he wished to fulfil before enjoying an overdue retirement from active service. He wanted to eclipse the tally of victories established by German ace Oswald Boelcke. Having achieved this ambition, he fully intended to return home, to his beloved Flora Young.

Oswald Boelcke was dead, killed in January 1917. His replacement was the Prussian aristocrat Manfred Von Richthofen. Oswald Boelcke had been Von Richthofen's commanding officer when, in August 1916, the Prussian had joined Jadgstaffle 2 a German fighter squadron. Like Albert Ball, his first victory had gone unconfirmed. But before long it was evident that Germany had a fighting progeny on its hands. Von Richthofen scored his first official victory in September 1916. After that he averaged a victory a week, a work rate he sustained until 1917. In November he shot down the English Ace Lanoe Hawker. Von Richthofen landed his own plane beside the downed aircraft and took a trophy, a habit that he would continue throughout the war. Unlike Ball he was a master technician in the air. With Boelcke dead, Von Richthofen took command of Jasta II, a new fighting unit. He flew an Albatross, as did his men. He painted his aircraft crimson and in time came to be known as the Red Baron.

The advent of the Red Baron and Jasta II ushered in a new level of intensity in aerial combat. April 1917 became known as Bloody April for the number of Royal Flying Corps pilots killed. Albert Ball survived the month and harvested victory after victory, dramatically increasing his total. He had been considered an extraordinary fighter pilot when his tally hovered around the dozen mark, just prior to his return home the previous October. Now his tally was somewhere approaching the forties. He had little left to prove. He had served out his month and ought to have gone home. But Albert Ball carried on fighting into early May and on the 7th, one year to the day since he had joined No. 11 Squadron, he was killed in action.

The exact circumstances surrounding his death are mysterious and may never be properly understood. Albert Ball was flying his second mission of the day, having already flown escort duty to bombers. His last mission was a patrol flight with ten other planes taken from three different flights. The patrol ran into enemy aircraft. There was a confusing and costly series of dog fights in which at least five Flying Corps pilots were killed. During the fray, Albert Ball chased an Albatross DIII into a cloud. The Albatross emerged from the cloud and crashed. Albert Ball came out of the cloud a short while later. His plane was upside down and flying toward the ground. When the plane hit the ground Albert Ball broke his arm and his back. He died moments later. No machine gun damage to his aircraft was visible. In all probability the cloud had disoriented him and he had flown out of it too low to be able to right his plane. The day before his death he had written a letter to Flora Young. In it he said, 'I am indeed looked after by God, but oh! I do get tired of always living to kill.'

Albert Ball was buried in grave J9 at Annoeulline on 9 May. Both Manfred Von Richtofen and his brother Lothar were credited with the kill. Neither was responsible. Mementos and trophies were stripped from Albert's aircraft and put on show in the Von Richtofen museum.

Above left: Albert Ball photographed in his fighter plane on the day of his death. (Courtesy of Nottingham City Council and www.picturethepast.org.uk)

Above right: The statue of Albert Ball in the grounds of Nottingham Castle.

Left: The plaque on Albert Ball's memorial statue lists his extraordinary military achievements.

Captain Ball's final tally rested at forty-four confirmed victories, exceeding Oswald Boelke by four kills. He would be posthumously awarded the Victoria Cross. A monument was erected at the chapel of Trent College where he had been educated. Albert Ball's father bought the land where he was buried. He also established eight alms houses in Lenton for widows of the First World War.

The most lasting memorial was the bronze statue by Henry Poole, of Albert Ball that still stands in the grounds of Nottingham Castle today. During statues unveiling Air Marshall Sir Hugh Trenchard said of the war hero, 'He made use of every minute of his crowded life.'